FIFTY
≡ Quick ≡
IDEAS

50quickideas.com

FIFTY
Quick
IDEAS

TO IMPROVE YOUR

RETRO
SPECTIVES

by
Tom Roden
&
Ben Williams

FIFTY QUICK IDEAS
TO IMPROVE YOUR RETROSPECTIVES

PRINT ISBN: **978-0-9930881-2-4**

Published on: 1. November 2015
Copyright © Neuri Consulting LLP
Authors: Tom Roden and Ben Williams
Copy-editor: Marjory Bisset
Design and layout: Nikola Korac

Many of the designations used by manufacturers and sellers to distinguish their products are claimed as trademarks. Where these designations appear in this book, and the publisher was aware of a trademark claim, the designations have been printed with initial capital letters or in all capitals.

The publisher has taken care in the preparation of this book, but makes no expressed or implied warranty of any kind and assumes no responsibility for errors or omissions. No liability is assumed for incidental or consequential damages in connection with or arising out of the use of the information or programs contained herein.

Published by:
Neuri Consulting LLP
25 Southampton Buildings
London WC2A2AL
United Kingdom

CONTENTS

It is the mark of a good action that it appears inevitable in retrospect

Robert Louis Stevenson

INTRODUCTION

About the book

Retrospectives have been the pulse of continuous improvement for teams since the boom in popularity of agile methods. For organisations who only inspected a project after it had delivered (or not), moving to a bi-weekly or monthly improvement cycle was a revolutionary shift, but why stop there? Unfortunately, many teams repeat the same process over and over so their retrospectives become flat, unrewarding and get discarded because they stop adding value. This can slow down improvement and demotivate team members.

Learn how to improve retrospectives and avoid stagnation, with fifty ideas designed to help you enhance and energise your continuous improvement effort. This book will help you get better outcomes from retrospectives and from any continuous improvement initiative. It will help you consider how best to prepare for retrospectives, generate innovative insights, achieve valuable outcomes, improve facilitation techniques, keep things fresh and maybe even how to have a bit of fun whilst doing it.

Who is this book for?

This book is for anyone who undertakes continuous improvement of any sort, especially those looking to get better outcomes from retrospectives, either as a participant, facilitator, coach or manager of teams. We include ideas for people with varying levels of experience. So, whether you are quite new to agile, Scrum and retrospectives, a veteran of continuous improvement looking to fine-tune or get new inspiration, or if your retrospectives have become a bit stale and need re-invigorating, there are ideas in here to support you.

Many of the ideas and concepts are universally applicable and will be of use to anyone trying to make improvements in any industry or walk of life. They are not limited to the confines of software development, where we work.

Who is this book not for?

This book is not for someone without any knowledge of retrospectives. We are making an assumption that our readers will understand what a retrospective is, as well as how to go about using them. If you have little or no experience participating in or facilitating retrospectives, please read another book first. There are plenty of good books and materials out there that introduce the basic processes and formats.

PREPARING FOR RETROSPECTIVES

COUNT YOUR INTERRUPTIONS

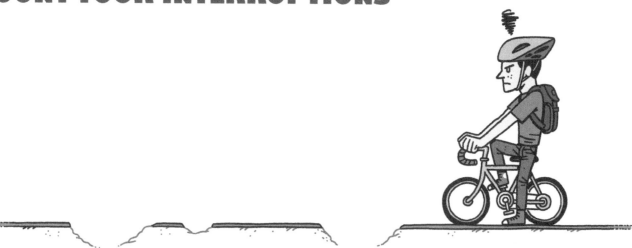

We all get distracted at work. If we had a pound for every time one of us got distracted while in the middle of something, then – well maybe that's an experiment to try out!

Open-plan offices are very popular these days. They tend to be noisy places and agile software development teams tend to create some pretty vocal environments. So when a number of teams are working closely in a department there are a fair few decibels and a lot of interaction. Context switching is taxing (literally). Moving between tasks and getting familiar with the new context takes time and grey matter, particularly when we are deeply immersed in knowledge work.

In the book *Peopleware: Productive Projects and Teams*, Timothy Lister and Tom DeMarco talk about the heavy cost of open-plan environments in terms of the sheer amount of distraction. Since they wrote that book, the number of distractions and the different types of interruptions have increased. Just think about the explosion of social media and the increased tendency of applications to make themselves known, such as Outlook flashing each email onto your screen as it arrives. Lister and DeMarco also describe a state that psychologists call 'flow', a state where a person is intensely focused on a task, time seems to fly and people can just burn through work. This state of being 'in the zone' (different to the state felt after a few pints of beer when one, usually misguidedly, feels unbeatable at pool) can take up to 15 minutes to reach. The research into flow also suggests that work needs to be challenging to take us into this state of intense concentration. A fair number of tasks in software, whether design, development or testing, are challenging. So distractions can cost a lot of wasted time, and therefore money.

The cost of distractions is made up of both the length of time we get distracted for and the absolute number of distractions we suffer. If you are getting distracted several times a day, or worse, several times an hour, the cost of losing where you were and having to immerse yourself back in the task again is very high.

Start to count your interruptions and distractions – it can be quite revealing, even shocking. Every time a member of the team is interrupted or distracted by something, count it. A person could do this on their own, but it works very well as a team activity. Count all the interruptions and distractions for a given period of time. This will give you some data to start analysing and using as part of the input to your retrospectives.

Key benefits

Just through measuring the interruptions, teams start to become really aware of quite how many times they get distracted. Teams start thinking about the associated cost, particularly when they are deeply engrossed in a piece of work.

This approach provides a visible way of measuring waste incurred through interruptions. It's a light-hearted approach too, which gives teams a better chance of sticking in teams' daily processes.

Collection provides a good source of data for input into retrospectives and for experiments with improvement ideas, especially if you break the interruptions down into types as described below.

Another great use for this data that we've found is that it helps teams to establish working patterns for quiet or interruptible time. That can be really helpful in a large department or project, working closely with many other teams. Having conversations with others about the best times for avoiding interruptions can lead to agreements on quiet time and lead to happier, more productive teams, synchronising their periods for immersion in the deep flow of working on challenging tasks.

How to make it work

It is hard to quantify losses of concentration in absolute terms, so there is possibly more value in the measure as a trend in the number of distractions. Once a baseline number of interruptions has been established, the team can then experiment with how to reduce them.

It is not easy to calculate an exact time lost per interruption. However, if we make an assumption that it takes 10 minutes (instead of 15, to err on the lower side) to settle into a task, we can make a fairly simple calculation of the cost we incur. For example, in a team of eight people, if each person is interrupted just 6 times a day, then that is 8 hours gone. A whole person, or 12.5% of the team's capacity, is wasted every single day. That is just by being interrupted, and does not include the time spent on the interruption itself.

The other key thing to decide on is how to record the data and to what level of detail. Try to keep the data visible and make the process light-hearted, so people remember to do it and are motivated. The simplest way is just a tally system on a whiteboard. Some teams favour more elaborate record-keeping, collecting other pieces of information like time of day, type of interruption, duration, what they were doing at the time and even the response they gave (an answer, pointing to documentation, teaching, 'wrong number').

Some physical action performed when a person moves between tasks can work well. A colleague of ours suggested that to make it more engaging for the team, they should throw pieces of Lego into a box using bricks of different colours for different categories of interruption. For example, red for a telephone call, white when a person comes to the team, blue when an email arrives, etc.

On a cautionary note, it's important to make sure people realise that counting interruptions is not about stopping communication between colleagues, or making it unacceptable for anyone to ask for help from another team. It is about identifying the unnecessary stuff and maybe rethinking the way in which we use the plethora of tools at our disposal. From a team perspective, it can still be desirable to put aside periods of time to work without any interruption at all, in order to enable members to focus on challenging tasks.

WALK THE VALUE STREAM

Teams who have been together and running retrospectives for a long time, continually looking for minor improvements in their internal processes, could be missing a key point. They should be thinking about some much bigger challenges, that will present themselves if people start to think more holistically.

If teams only focus on things in their immediate sphere of influence, they will get to the point where they feel like an explorer dying of thirst, trying to get the last few drops of water from her canteen, while a raging river gushes along, audible, yet frustratingly out of sight.

As the returns for improvement efforts get lower and lower, some people can start to question the value of retrospectives. Ultimately, some teams start to skip retrospectives. Continuous improvement is far too important to just skip.

The theory of constraints, as described by Eli Goldratt in *The Goal: A Process of Ongoing Improvement*, notes that the continual local optimisation of one part of a value stream over others is actually detrimental to the overall flow of a product. Practically, if we tune our car engine without considering the fact that we have fitted bicycle wheels, we are not likely to see any improvement, or worse, we will overload the wheels and blow up the system.

In order to find fresh improvement ideas, teams need to expand the horizons of their continuous improvement effort. One of the most effective ways for this is by walking the value stream. Factory managers might be able to literally walk along a part of the value stream within a production line, but in software development we have to do this virtually.

This requires a shift of thinking for many teams. It is essentially refocusing the team from its own boundaries to considering the flow of work all the way from concept to cash. Put another way, it is shifting focus from the silo that the team works in to a view of the world through the eyes of the work.

Key benefits

When teams consider the whole value stream, they become more aware of the bigger picture, gaining a new appreciation for why they do what they do, and where they fit in. People refocus from having the most efficient development capability on improving the overall flow of the product. Teams retrospecting in this manner will have a much larger target for improvement ideas. Teams inspecting their value streams are no longer looking for team problems, they are looking for work problems.

Before trying this approach, teams might have thought they just had to live with problems up and down the value stream. But as the artist Banksy has tweeted, 'The most dangerous phrase in language is *we've always done it this way*'.

By broadening their horizons, teams will ultimately change the relationships across their whole business. They will improve relationships that have in the past been contractual, creating a desire to work together to deliver throughout the value stream. Jeff Patton once said that 'nobody likes to disappoint a friend'.

How to make it work

We like the analogy that the work is a car on a journey and the team members are passengers in that car. What do they see? What stoppages and diversions do they experience? What energy do they waste bringing the car to a standstill and speeding back up again?

We use a technique to simulate the journey of the work similar to value stream mapping. Find the start point for each piece of work. This is not the point at which the team receives a request, but the point at which the need was identified. Follow that need through the value stream, noting all the things that happened along the way. Note the durations of individual stages, both active and waiting, and also all the different people involved. This information should provide the team with plenty of fresh improvement ideas.

When walking the value stream, the team should select a few pieces of work that they have recently completed. Use a typical piece of work for improving the general workflow, for example, how the value

stream is arranged, how work is prioritised and how it is batched for release. Ideas generated from these pieces of work help change the normal way of doing things. Also select a painful piece of work. This will enable teams to improve the less frequent but high cost problems, specific to certain types of work. Think of rogue dependencies and false assumptions.

Teams need to expand their influence to areas outside of their immediate control. This can be achieved by using quantitative data to create business cases and also qualitative techniques such as improving relationships with customers and suppliers, both external and internal.

The ultimate use of this retrospective technique is to involve all the members of the value stream. Having everyone present provides not only agreement on *what* happened but also a greater understanding as to *why* something happened. For example, *why* did the work sit waiting for 8 days? In addition, having an open dialogue about the flow of work, rather than the people involved, depersonalises insights and avoids criticism. This encourages improvement of the system as a whole.

USE NUMBERS TO GAUGE SUCCESS

When a team is asked if their last improvement idea was a success, we quite commonly hear answers such as 'Yes, I think so', 'Erm...not sure' or 'I think we are working better'. People are drawing conclusions from their gut feelings. There is no specific evidence to vindicate sustaining the change in working methods.

Teams and stakeholders often question the value of retrospectives. If the only thing people can say when challenged is 'we think we got better', we are losing valuable information about the real effects of improvement ideas. Even within the same team, different members often have different points of view about the relative merit of an improvement idea. This can be a source of discord amongst the team members, because their views are often not based on hard data.

Think back to high school science. We were taught to present a hypothesis, test that hypothesis and then conclude whether it was correct or not. Now we are all older and oh so much wiser, why is it that we seem to have forgotten this?

In order to better judge the impact of proposed changes, add a measure of success to your improvement ideas (your hypothesis). By adding a measure of success, you can more accurately conclude whether the idea was a success.

Key benefits

Adding a measure of success provides focus in two ways. Firstly, it provides focus in the room as the team members form their improvement idea. This is useful for many teams, as it exposes ambiguity about exactly what they are trying to achieve. Secondly, it helps make sure they reach a shared understanding of their goal.

Tom once worked with a team who wanted to improve their build pipeline. For this idea, each team member left the room nodding and agreeing that they knew exactly what they were aiming for. At some point during the next iteration, there came a revelation. Two different pairs of team members had both been improving the build pipeline. They had been improving the builds for completely different components. In the next retrospective, the team tried again, but also agreed on a specific measure of success: to make the whole build for one component run in less than 30 minutes. Simply using numbers to pin down the specifics of the improvement was enough to build shared understanding, and avoid working on the wrong things.

When the goal and measures are posted in the team area, the team can see them during their daily stand-up. Team members can see visible progress towards them and be reminded of their commitment to continuously improve. A practice we like to use for this is to add the goal on to any information or feedback radiators the team is using e.g. cumulative flow diagrams, burnups, metrics dashboard.

Having a measure of success means it is possible to talk about the value of continuous improvement with real data to back it up, and thus justify the time spent on continuous improvement. Measures of success allow teams to say things like 'we have removed five hours of waste per release with this improvement idea'. Validated numbers allow people to champion their efforts outside the team, by providing data about real tangible improvements that they can talk about. The

team gets credit from peers and management, whilst inspiring others to improve in this way. The same process also helps within the team when the value of continuous improvement is scrutinised.

How to make it work

During the retrospective session, as the team members formulate an improvement idea, make sure that the focus is on what success would look like and how to measure it.

To conclude whether something has improved, we need a number of inputs. We need to know what to measure, how to measure it, what the baseline is now and at what point in the future the measurement is to be taken. It is also useful to have a target level that shows success. Try using the Deming cycle of Plan, Do, Check, Act (PDCA) in conjunction with Toyota's 'A3' problem solving and continuous improvement technique. Other teams find it useful to use SMART goals (Small, Measurable, Attainable, Relevant, Time-bound) to frame their improvement ideas.

Many teams will argue that it is practically impossible to measure some desirable outcomes. For example, it is difficult to gauge 'deliver more business value' or 'improve team effectiveness'. In *How to Measure Anything*, Doug Hubbard says that anything you can observe, you can measure.

For example, a team we worked with wanted to implement the decider protocol, a technique for decision-making described by McCarthy and McCarthy in *Software for Your Head*, so that they reduce contention within the team. We asked them to think about how they could spot contention. Two common symptoms were arguments and people choosing to work from home. Both are measurable.

Be aware that a single measure by itself does not tell the complete story. If you see an improvement in a chosen metric, this might seem like success. But if it has been achieved at the expense of something else that the team values, inspect the situation closer. Is the trade-off acceptable? Check for possible adverse consequences of improvements.

TAKE DATA INTO THE ROOM

There are two important drawbacks when teams start retrospectives with a blank slate:

- Grounding and gathering data consumes time
- When people gather data from memory, the process is much more susceptible to bias and subjectivity

Negativity bias can be particularly toxic in retrospectives, since individuals find it easier to recall negative memories over positive. The result is a disproportionately high number of negative retrospective sessions, which in turn depress the team's mood and morale.

The effect of confirmation bias is equally harmful. Confirmation bias is explained in depth by Daniel Kahneman in *Thinking, Fast and Slow*. Using intuition (and not data), team members are likely to recall events that are in line with what they believe already happened. Ultimately, this means that teams often fail to explore the facts using data in favour of staying with the comfort of their gut reactions.

Bringing data into the room for retrospective sessions helps us avoid these problems. We commonly use iteration burn-down charts, the team board, release burn-up charts and plans, pairing ladders, waste snakes and the stories and tasks the team members recently worked on. Any data can be useful, even about the product we are working towards.

Key benefits

Data-driven artefacts lend themselves to being used as both inputs to the retrospective session and as measures for potential improvement ideas.

Taking data into a retrospective session immediately saves time. Instead of recalling and gathering the data about the previous iteration, the team might use the time to generate improvement ideas. The resulting insights are more likely to reflect reality than those driven by gut instinct.

Real data forms ready-made measures from which to judge the relative success of the improvement ideas.

Using this technique brings about a new appreciation for artefacts that, in the past, teams might have prepared by rote and without a critical eye. Some new teams start out with a cargo-cult attitude, believing that just producing the artefacts will improve their process. When the artefacts are used to generate insights, teams understand better the value of those artefacts, and start targeting specific measures for improvement.

How to make it work

Most agile teams have a visual display board for work, where they focus during daily stand-ups. This information radiator is a perfect source of data for the team retrospective. If your team board is mobile, wheel it into the retrospective room. If the board is immobile, use a laptop and projector to display pictures of the board in the retrospective room. Alternatively, take artefacts from the board into the room. Unfinished tasks, waste snakes and release plans printed on paper can be useful for starting a retrospective.

Focus attention on those artefacts that radiate information critical to the team at that point in time. Release plans or a burn-up chart are a useful prompt for teams approaching a delivery date. Artefacts that measure quality, such as defect density graphs or defect counts over time, are useful for teams who focus on extrinsic quality. The trick here is to bring data relevant to your team and context at that point in time.

Ben worked with a team that took this idea one step further. The team members were continually over-committing to work. At the end of each sprint, they often had unfinished tasks, and they could not work out why. To shed some light on the situation, the team decided to take a picture of their team board each day of the iteration, to see if they could spot any patterns. At the end of the iteration, the team flipped back and forth through the photos for a while, before one team member actually took the photos and combined them into a short time-lapse video clip. During the next retrospective, the whole team watched as, one by one, all their tasks moved into the 'progress' column, but very few moved to 'done'. The outcome of that retrospective was that they decided to 'stop starting and start finishing', through being more disciplined over work-in-progress limits.

Any artefact can be used in two ways: it can just provide (part of) the context for generating insights, or it can itself form the basis for an improvement hypothesis. In the latter case, an artefact provides the data and the measure of success, as explored in the section *Use numbers to gauge success*.

Finally, having the physical board in front of your team allows you to annotate the data there and then. We have worked with teams who would annotate notes during the iteration, and then read back the notes at the start of the retrospective. Mark expected results of improvement ideas directly onto charts, so that the team can focus on these during the next iteration.

CROWD-SOURCE FEEDBACK

Getting to the root of problems can be very hard for teams, regardless of whether they have just formed or have been together for years. Digging into issues takes significant effort and can be both uncomfortable and unnatural for many people.

No matter how diligent a retrospective process is, an isolated team may subconsciously or even consciously choose to avoid difficult issues – essentially avoiding the elephant in the room.

Even if the team attacks the issues head on, they might benefit from an external perspective. Independent observers might spot problems that the team is falling foul of, or see patterns they have become blind to, in a typical case of not seeing the wood for the trees.

A good solution for this is to ask others for their views. Make the artefacts you use to retrospect available to other people you work alongside and ask for their opinion. Ask them for observations, commentary, patterns they might see that will help the team improve. Consider offering the opportunity to provide feedback anonymously.

Key benefits

Widening the target audience for gathering feedback and ideas enables a team to obtain a huge amount of insight into their way of working. Drawing on the diverse range and levels of experience of surrounding people will yield richer and deeper insights than just using the team's own views.

The cost to the team of doing this is relatively low. It just requires a small amount of preparation and for you to be brave and open to negative feedback.

Crowd-sourcing feedback gives a team fresh eyes on the situation. The independence of the commenters and the sheer number of people contributing are very likely to lead to them spotting something that the team itself might have missed.

If, in addition, you choose to have that feedback given anonymously, you will encourage honest and critical comments without any sugar-coating. Such feedback could otherwise be inhibited for fear of upsetting the team, especially in larger organisations.

How to make it work

The key to getting good crowd-sourced feedback is to make it as easy as possible for people to suggest improvements. The easier it is to provide feedback, the more information you will receive. The most effective method we have seen is to print things off and put them somewhere prominent.

Take your dashboard, print it out and stick it on the wall. Your dashboard could consist of your cumulative flow diagram, burn-down or burn-up charts, quality and delivery statistics, ways of working or any other artefact that you collect and use. This will enable others to take a look at the data and generate some insights. Think of it like a doctor reading your medical charts.

Put the artefacts in a place that people regularly walk past or visit to discuss their own problems with each other – this is perfect water-cooler territory. Put them on a wall with a big sign inviting feedback. Tape a pencil or marker to a string alongside the board to make feedback as frictionless as possible.

Leave the data up for a week and invite people to comment by annotating the artefacts directly. Inviting people to comment anonymously will make them more likely to offer critical feedback. The feedback won't be much use if you can't read their writing or understand their points so ask people to write clearly.

Make it clear that you are soliciting constructive feedback about problems that people see in the data and not solutions to perceived problems. Encourage feedback that points out an issue, such as 'it looks like you have a bottleneck here' rather than makes a diagnosis, such as 'this decrease in quality is probably due to the stress the team is under and I would invest in removing technical debt'. The former gives us information on which to retrospect and make a judgment in our context, while with the latter the person assumes they already know our context and jumps to a proposed solution.

Even when they have been invited we've found that people hesitate to be the first to deface an artefact by adding a comment. Get the ball rolling by providing some annotations of your own. This should open the floodgates to wider feedback.

Take the annotated artefacts into your retrospective session. Invite all the team members to review the content silently at the same time. Once they have had the chance to digest the information, they can then discuss some of the points raised.

We have used open discussion for this part or had the team members vote by putting sticky dots directly next to the feedback item they would like to discuss further.

A word of warning though, remember this feedback is generated based on the data that the individual had at that point in time. There are two things to be aware of. If a commenter has additional knowledge of what is going on in your team, for example they recently overheard a heated discussion, this could cause them to provide advice instead of reflecting on the data. If the quality and scope of the data you provided is limited, the assertions made in the feedback could mislead you.

A safe stance to take is to remember that the team knows its own context better than anyone else, so if the comment presumes to know something that doesn't really resonate with the team, discard it and move onto the next.

VISUALISE WASTE

A strict definition of waste in the agile development world is that it is anything that doesn't add value in the eyes of the customer. Larman and Vodde assert in their book *Scaling Lean and Agile Development* that over 90% of lead time can be defined as waste and our own adventures with value stream mapping have found similar levels. There is clearly enormous potential for improvement by removing waste.

So what blocks people from seeing all this waste? It can be tempting to believe that waste is inevitable or 'just the way things are' and accept or overlook it. The longer the time spent working within a system, the harder it becomes to see the waste as removable or temporary. Identifying waste is a great idea, but not many teams we've seen consistently do it, and fewer still quantify or categorise it.

We've observed that teams often lack a consistent way to trigger the identification of waste. They also often lack a way of categorising, quantifying and monitoring the wasteful work that they identify. Once teams start identifying waste though, it can come as a surprise that they start to see it everywhere they look and might ask 'Where did all this waste come from?'. Arnold M. Zwicky, a professor of linguistics at Stanford University, coined two terms that explain this. Firstly, the Recency Illusion describes a selective attention effect where one believes that things noticed only recently, actually occurred recently. Secondly, the Frequency Illusion describes how becoming aware of something skews our estimates of frequency as we become aware of every occurrence. On the Internet, a more popular name for this is the Baader-Meinhof phenomenon, from a famous comment about the namesake German terrorist group at the St. Paul Pioneer Press' online discussion board. In fact it is likely that a lot of this waste has been present for some time, only now the light has been switched on to see it.

To make delivery more efficient it is essential to release the brakes that waste places on improvement. Capture waste as an input for your retrospective by setting up a visual cue such as a waste snake or waste bin, which will prompt team members to add items and tackle them.

Key benefits

Visualising waste is particularly helpful for teams that have become stuck in the same way of working for years and 'can't see the wood for the trees'. They might not even be aware of the problems and constraints caused by the environment. Putting wasteful activities on a wall helps to make people aware of the extent of it, and demonstrates that it is okay to highlight waste.

Even when people already identify and capture waste, they often don't go so far as to quantify the levels. Adding the impact of the waste, say by calculating the amount of time lost and number of people impacted by each wasteful activity, enables you to put a concrete value on each individual item. As an input to your retrospective session, this is incredibly useful information. You can assess how much it is worthwhile spending to remove it and over what period you would recover the money. This in turn can inform a business case with which to assess experiments to run in order to try to remove the waste cost-effectively.

The action of writing and placing another sticky note on the board can be quite cathartic. Teams who have diligently used a waste snake have wound the body

completely round the board within a two-week period. So expect something resembling a giant anaconda to emerge pretty quickly and don't worry as that's normal.

How to make it work

The key to making this an effective practice is maintaining the discipline to keep collecting and removing waste, both large and small instances of it. Firstly, find a good space to visualise the waste in the system, such as a whiteboard. Tip – you'll need more space than you think.

To use a waste snake, draw the head of the snake and then use sticky notes containing a description of each piece of waste to fill out its body. Quantify each item, such as how many hours lost, how many people affected, and possibly categorise it to allow more detailed inspection. Each day when you visit your board use the snake as a prompt to ask yourselves, 'what waste did I experience yesterday?'. Continue to add sticky notes to create the body of the snake, winding it around your board.

When you start the next retrospective session, there will be some great data to analyse and inform improvement ideas. Take all the sticky notes into your retrospective session and place them up on the walls. Have the team put them into groups of similar items and then total the amount of waste for each group. Think about how you are going to prioritise and manage the groups, and what experiments you are going to run to try and remove the waste. There will likely be some big themes to tackle, or you might decide first to tackle some smaller, but still impactful waste.

Instead of a waste snake you could consider using a waste bin. The advantage of a bin is that it provides a prioritisation system. Draw the bin with two axes, one for the impact of the waste on the team (maybe low-high or even quantified in some more objective way) and one for the cost to remove (again low-high or time required to remove). Then the team members effectively prioritise the waste items as they add them to the board. It makes sense to tackle items that have a high cost to the team but a low cost of removal before those with a low cost to the team and a high cost of removal.

RUN AN IDEAS BOX

For teams retrospecting on a longer period of time, accurately recalling events can be hard. This is of particular consequence to teams reflecting after a major delivery milestone. If we can't faithfully recall what mattered, we'll lack some valuable data on which to base observations. Actually, from our own personal experiences, even remembering the events of the last two weeks can be difficult.

As discussed in *Take data into the room*, relying upon recalling events from memory leaves teams susceptible to several biases. These biases mean that potentially important improvement areas can be left unexplored.

To avoid missing important data, collect information as you go along. Set up an ideas box and let people add events, thoughts, observations and ideas as they occur.

Key benefits

If you have more information of different types to retrospect upon, you will get a broader spectrum of retrospection topics and ultimately a more diverse set of potential improvement ideas. You also avoid many biases.

Having actual data in the retrospective provides a more accurate account of the topic on which the team is retrospecting. This helps to avoid the effect of rose-tinted glasses – remembering things more positively because they are in the past. The data also helps people to avoid exaggerating issues.

An ideas box helps you to keep retrospectives shorter because there is no need to recall events and data from the past time period. Instead there is a pool of data ready to classify and retrospect upon.

Prompting the immediate capture of ideas is the first step to achieving continuous retrospection, discussed in the section *Don't batch your retrospection*.

How to make it work

Find an old box with a lid and cut a hole in the top big enough for folded paper to pass through. For bonus points, wrap it in some distinguishing paper to attract attention to it and remind people of its existence throughout the sprint. Tape the lid closed. We have found that this enables people to contribute their content in relative safety. Make the process anonymous to start with. People will not feel inhibited by the thought that they will have to publicly share their observation. With anonymity, some context might be missing when it is time to discuss the observation. To avoid this encourage more detail on the original submission.

Before you encourage people to add content, establish some ground rules with the team. Consider whether people outside the team can put ideas into the box. This can provide deeper insight into events that a team's stakeholders think is important. Be aware that ideas can be taken out of context if they are not personally introduced at retrospective time. Ask stakeholders to be aware of this as they write their submissions.

Once in place, encourage people to add content to the box as things happen. Try prompting people during the daily stand-up. This can be done conveniently when

Empty the box out in the retrospective. Get the team members to take it in turn to describe the content that they added and why. As the team sort through the content, they can group it into piles for similar themes. The simplest way to move forward would be to vote on a theme to discuss in more detail. This method can be used as a building block to gather data with many other published retrospective formats.

Beware of too much data. If team members are adding too much content to the box, it will take a long time to sort at the start of the retrospective. If this happens, try having the facilitator sort and theme the content ahead of time. Alternatively limit the amount of content that each person can add per day. Try having people add a piece of content just at the daily stand-up.

they recall what they did the previous day. Eventually, adding content to the box will become so ingrained that team members will do this naturally at various points throughout the day.

Encourage team members to add different types of content. It is nice to have a thank-you note for a job well done. It is also very interesting to have actual artefacts from the development process. We facilitated a retrospective where a team member had printed off a chart showing plots of opened and closed defects and put it into the ideas box. When the box was opened the chart attracted a lot of discussion. The plots of open and closed defects narrowed significantly over time. This was useful feedback on the team's effort to reduce outstanding defects and led to an action to increase their effort in the coming sprint.

One thing we learnt along the way is to allow personalisation and humour to be included. This can really help team dynamics and bind the team together by sharing some funny ideas or comments they came up with.

It can also be powerful for people to personally retrospect on something that they added in the heat of the moment. We have experienced many retrospectives where team members have asked to withdraw an observation that over time has become less important to them. Often team members subsequently learn something that changes their opinion on a matter. When team members have the space to silently retrospect on their submissions, they often learn to have more patience with one another. They understand that perspectives and levels of understanding change with time.

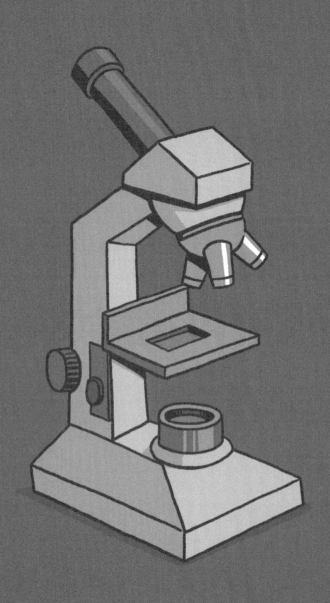

FIFTY
Quick
IDEAS

PROVIDING A CLEAR FOCUS

RENEW YOUR VOWS

As a team, it is valuable to establish some common values or ways of working, and to write them down as a team charter. However, even when written down, it is not uncommon for them to become out of date and unused over a longer period of time.

Often when teams form they are buoyed by the chance of success, the opportunity to do something great, to work with new people. In this frame of mind they resolve to be disciplined in practice and process, and at this point they choose to establish and write down these common values and principles.

Such rules help the team self-regulate, rather than relying on a scrum meddler (scrum master if you prefer). You know the kind of thing: 'We will all turn up for stand-up on time' and 'We will pre-arrange working from home'. They will be displayed in the team area, laminated maybe, with the intention the team will police itself by referring to them.

Over time though, the team members forget the qualities they once held dear. Experience of working with many teams has taught us some valuable lessons, for example, that even excellent teams can lose sight of their principles. Once team members stop conforming to the rules they initially established, they no longer know what to expect from one another, which can have damaging consequences.

Retrospect on your team's ways of working or team charter on a regular basis to refresh what principles and behaviours you value, where you've been slipping, and what changes you need to make in order to align yourselves back to you team philosophy.

Key benefits

A formalised set of gudelines in a team charter gives team members something independent to reference so they can keep themselves in check. It is a kind of true north if you will, guiding the team through difficult times and decisions. When things get heated or if someone feels they are being unfairly treated, referring back to the team's charter can be much more objective than letting emotions distort facts. Ultimately this should mean that the team becomes less reliant on the scrum master or facilitator.

If your retrospective sessions gravitate towards technical improvements, using the team charter is a great way to generate improvements on how the team works together. Repeated at intervals, this retrospective session makes sure the team holds to, reviews and refines the values they consider important. It ensures that the team's ways of working stay up to date.

Level setting each team member's expectation of one another helps diffuse situations before problems arise. In our experience, team conflicts result from a mismatch in expectation rather than a lack of respect for one another. Retrospecting on the team charter on a regular basis helps avoid that mismatch.

Renewal of vows is a positive thing. It reminds the team of the feeling they had when the first set their team charter, and how they have evolved since they last revisited their ways of working.

How to make it work

Firstly, if you don't have a team charter or way of working then use one of your retrospective sessions to create one. Creating one will force your team to answer fundamental questions about what you value as a team, while reaching shared understanding about how to behave and interact with each other.

Once you've been using a team charter for a while, say after a few months or maybe when you start a new milestone or chunk of work, spend one of your sessions reviewing its contents.

At the review go through each of the points in your charter and ask yourself as a team:

- 'Are we still following this principle?'
- If yes, 'Do we still need an explicit rule?'
- If not, 'Is it still important to us?'
- Is there anything we want to add based on the problems we have?

Review the team's broad policies and all the processes used in estimation, planning, analysis, and so on. At this point, it is not uncommon for team members to disagree about whether they feel a rule should be kept or not. For example, the team might all agree that they are very good at turning up to meetings on time and others point it out when they are late. Some might therefore propose that the rule be deleted. Others however, might fear that removal of the rule would result in a deterioration in time-keeping.

Our experience is that it is often preferable to keep a rule, so if in doubt err on the side of caution – if you are concerned that removing a rule will make the situation worse, keep it.

It is imperative to get consensus, otherwise the charter is liable to fail in its purpose. If you find rules that are implicitly followed and no longer a point of contention, then remove any physical reminders and triggers. This is a sign of a maturing team. The point is that the rules are there to help the team and only the team, if a rule is no longer important there is no need to keep it.

Obviously, adding and removing rules should not have to wait for the next retrospective. As with all continuous improvement, feel free to amend this living document on the fly, but always get consensus.

It's important to ensure the charter is easy to maintain and use. In *The Checklist Manifesto*, Atul Gawande says that lists of more than nine items tend to become unmanageable and are less likely to be used.

FOCUS ON STAKEHOLDER RELATIONSHIPS

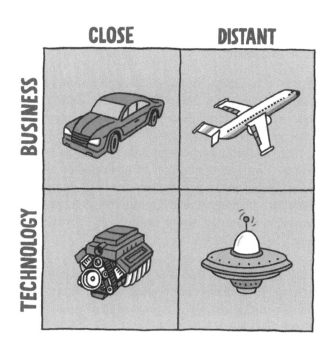

How many times do teams in your company include stakeholders from outside the team in their retrospectives? Do they run retrospectives that focus on relationships with stakeholders?

Teams who regularly include their product owner in retrospectives naturally discuss challenges relating to that relationship sometimes. As discussed in *Involve business stakeholders*, physical (or virtual) presence and sharing problems shows a degree of openness that builds trust in the relationship between team and product owner. Yet very few teams we've met regularly invite stakeholders other than the product owner to retrospectives as a standard practice. This could be for various reasons – a tendency to focus on the more controllable aspects of the environment, or a case of 'out of sight, out of mind'. It could even be an indirect result of the emphasis agile methods place on the team. Whatever the reason, one consequence is that few retrospectives have a primary focus on stakeholder relationships.

Team–stakeholder relationships usually only get discussed when they have fallen into disrepair. Trying to fix them once they have deteriorated is topsy-turvy and will arguably take more effort than regular maintenance.

Don't leave the health of relationships down to chance and the goodwill of a few people. Spend time specifically working to maintain and improve your stakeholder relationships by devoting a retrospective session solely to them.

Key benefits

Regularly focusing on relationships means the team members understand the needs and perspective of their stakeholders. This understanding should make it easier to communicate ideas and needs, making interactions more efficient and effective, while also reducing barriers in hand-offs along the flow of work.

By considering the perspective of others the team members gain a broader understanding of others' needs. They learn to take a more holistic perspective that reduces the risk of only considering the team's needs and making purely local optimisations.

When the team needs help from outside in order to remove obstacles, having a better network of relationships and friends is invaluable. This applies particularly in larger and more dispersed organisations.

How to make it work

Once every three months have a retrospective session in which you focus on all the different stakeholders of the team. Understand what their main needs from the team are and what main services they give the team. Discuss how healthy the relationship is, how it could be improved and any potential problems.

Start by writing down all the specific stakeholders that the team has. Make sure you think about broad stakeholder groups, not just the product owner and anyone immediately upstream or downstream of the team. We have developed the 'know your stakeholder' quadrants to divide them into different categories. Have quadrants for:

- *Close proximity in technology:* this might include teams that you work alongside on your delivery.
- *Close proximity in business:* this will hopefully include your product owner and sponsors.
- *More distant in technology:* this could include teams in other departments that might integrate with your systems and components.
- *More distant in business:* this could include teams such as human resources and marketing.

Alternatively you could use the flow of the product to consider all the people involved in the value stream.

You can end up with a much larger set of stakeholders than you expected, but they are not all equal in terms of the amount of interaction required. You probably don't have time to assess each of these relationships at length, so triage the list.

Once you have done this, the next step is to generate insights into the nature and health of the relationships. Discuss areas of interest and decide on any actions to improve them. There are several approaches you could take. Here are some options we have found work well:

- Run a SWOT analysis on each relationship. Discuss strengths, weaknesses, opportunities (to improve the relationship) and threats (to the relationship).
- Answer the same set of questions for each stakeholder group, for example how frequently you meet, how many people interact in the relationship, what media you use to communicate. Rate the strength of relationship from 1 to 5.
- Work out a set of criteria for assessing stakeholder relationships, then perform an assessment for each one using the criteria. Use a scale (say 1-10) to help you identify the areas to focus on.
- Run a survey directly with your stakeholders to canvas their thoughts. Use a predefined set of questions (some teams we know have even used a net-promoter-score survey) or just ask for open-ended feedback.

The point of assessing the relationships is to identify those that require work in order to follow up with those stakeholders, not just analyse how to improve the relationship in isolation. Once you know which relationships need the most work, invite stakeholders to specific sessions. You might have a session for each type or combine those who you think are similar enough that their shared participation will benefit all involved. When you arrange the session make sure it is very clear that this is an opportunity to get better, it is not about assigning blame or a chance to moan. You will often need to plan well ahead to get the desired attendance.

HOLD A TECHNICAL DEBT RETROSPECTIVE

The concept of technical debt, defined by Ward Cunningham, is wonderful because it resonates easily with non-technical stakeholders. It describes shortcuts and design compromises that increase long-term cost and risk for short-term gain. Most teams today know about technical debt and occasionally try to reduce it. However, it's very rare to find teams that formally identify technical debt, measure it or track its removal. Because debt mostly stays under the radar, teams can't be sure how much it is affecting them, if it is reducing or increasing, or how much risk they are exposed to.

The time-to-market value of a product release can outweigh the risk and cost associated with design shortcuts, so increasing technical debt can be perfectly justifiable in the short run. But the aggregated effect of such choices has a significant impact on team productivity and the long-term product support effort. Although you can't measure precisely the impact of technical debt on team productivity, you can certainly identify it, quantify it and create a realistic plan to reduce it. Don't let debt quietly build up and remain unaddressed until it is a major problem. Hold a technical debt repayment retrospective to keep on top of it, and agree a repayment plan.

Key benefits

Surfacing and quantifying technical debt enables teams to estimate the risk it represents and to monitor it over time. This promotes awareness and responsibility in the team for managing debt and keeping it to acceptable levels. It also fosters healthy discussions about different approaches to design. Holding periodic technical debt retrospectives ensures it gets attention and doesn't accumulate unnoticed.

When the impact, risk and cost of technical debt are quantified, teams can have a more transparent discussion about design choices with business sponsors. The team can present risks in terms the sponsors can appreciate, instead of asking for 'two months to refactor the flux capacitor to use it as a micro-service'. This makes it easier to agree on the importance of reducing debt compared to working on new features, and helps to create a repayment plan. When a team continually collects and quantifies information about technical debt, business sponsors will become increasingly aware of the impact of delivery choices. Decision makers will better understand the trade-offs behind design shortcuts, yielding more considered decisions.

Debt repayment plans highlight the potential risk of current shortcuts, indicating if it is being satisfactorily addressed. These repayment plans allow everyone to see the reasons for investing in internal product quality or process improvements.

How to make it work

Start by capturing all the pieces of technical debt that people can think of. Although technical debt is most commonly associated with software design, we like to include any deviations from good engineering practices that could represent a potential future risk. This includes testing and process concerns. For example, if a team is aiming to implement a continuous delivery model but they decide to skip automating a part of the build pipeline, that decision should be included in technical debt.

Use Martin Fowler's *Technical Debt Quadrants* to drive the discussion. Draw one axis to divide the deliberate choices from the inadvertent – this describes the degree of consciousness while accruing the debt. Draw the other axis to divide the reckless from the prudent choices – this describes the degree of risk. Here is a brief introduction to each quadrant:

- *Deliberate prudent*: the team understood and acknowledged that the item would increase technical debt. They consciously chose to go ahead, because the short-term gains justified the risk and the cost of paying it back later.
- *Deliberate reckless*: the team took on debt to release faster, knowing that the choice might be sub-optimal but without really understanding the risks. This includes items that people thought might not need to be paid off, such as experimental or temporary features that stuck around.
- *Inadvertent prudent*: the team used sound practices, but despite this, changes in the business domain and learning through delivery have revealed better design options.
- *Inadvertent reckless*: the team did not understand at the time that they were making a poor decision.

Get the team members to write down ideas on sticky notes and place them in the appropriate quadrant. This approach challenges people to think beyond easily recognisable items, and explore less obvious problems.

Next, quantify the debt so the stakeholders can prioritise its removal. Think of each piece of debt in the same way as any other loan. There is the principal amount to pay back and the possibility of interest payments at a specific frequency. Unfortunately there is also the risk of default and even bankruptcy if the debt is severe enough! For example, if the technical

debt item is related to manually running tests that should have been automated, the principal amount is the time it would take to properly automate those tests. The interest payment is the time it takes to execute the tests manually, and the frequency of payment is how often the team needs to run those tests. The team may choose to default on the debt and not run those tests any more, but this carries a risk that a defect may occur, which could prove to be costly.

Next, prioritise the debt items and agree with the stakeholders which of them need to be resolved soon. Be aware that the the principal might change over time. Automating the missing tests immediately might be cheaper than a few months later, when the underlying code changes. So don't trust these estimates over long periods of time – run the technical debt retrospective periodically to keep on top of the problems.

USE TIMELINES WITH DIFFERENT DIMENSIONS

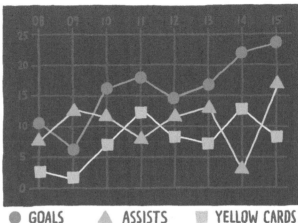

● GOALS ▲ ASSISTS ■ YELLOW CARDS

Generating insights can be tough for a team that has been working in the same environment on the same product and with the same people for a prolonged period of time. Sprints start to blur into one and if a team moves away from a fixed time-box method such as Scrum, there is even less with which to punctuate the passing of time. For longer periods of retrospection (such as a whole project) teams can struggle to focus on all the events, forgetting those things that happened in the distant past in favour of more recent events. This can limit the number and value of the improvement ideas they come up with. In addition, during retrospectives some teams tend to focus much more on 'harder' aspects such as tools, technologies and processes, and less on the 'softer', more human side.

In order to help teams retrospect and generate ideas for discussion, have the team complete a timeline of the period with different dimensions. Map out the major events that took place along the timeline, then overlay each individual's emotional state on top. To generate more effective insights, also consider adding a number of other dimensions including delivery and quality.

Key benefits

Using this technique provides a larger canvas of prompts from which to generate insights. Including different factors that affect the team provides a much clearer recollection of past occurrences, which drives out a diverse set of improvement ideas.

Overlaying the team members' emotional states gives a very different type of information with which to retrospect. Often we might miss the opportunity to retrospect on how the data-driven insights correlate with the emotional well-being of the team. Emotional and factual aspects provide a complete picture.

In addition, adding individuals' emotional states to the input data allows the team to retrospect on the differences between certain team members at certain points in time. Seeing the differences in team members' emotions at different times and in reaction to different events encourages them to appreciate how other people work and what makes them tick.

If we repeat this retrospective format at periodic intervals and compare current to historical depictions, then we can see trends over time. Visualising the team motivation changing over time, can be particularly fruitful to retrospect on.

Finally, it also allows people to represent how they were feeling without having to actually talk about the F-word (feelings).

How to make it work

Start by setting your time frame. This idea can be used as effectively for a two-week sprint as it can for a project retrospective spanning many months (although this requires more preparation and digging for dates). You need to create a long horizontal timeline, marking the start and end points of the period on which you would like to retrospect.

Practically, you can achieve this using a large whiteboard. If you only have access to painted wall space then try using lining wallpaper, rolled out horizontally and taped to the wall. Even large windows make a great canvas for sticky notes and also work well with whiteboard markers. Choose dark colours as they are more visible than light colours when used directly on the window.

Now spend some time to mark some significant points in time on the timeline. First delivery to production, a recent meeting with the client or setbacks such as environment downtime or system outages are all good prompts. Try not to discuss them in much detail at first (just what happened and the outcome or setback or time lost).

However, don't just stick to work-centric things. Use any dimensions that will trigger recollection of the period, for example a team night out, sickness or even curry day in the canteen.

Now try and overlay other data onto the timeline. If you have measures such as your burn-down or burn-up charts, production defects, support incidents or maybe even usage metrics of the product over the length of a project, then have this data mapped onto the timeline.

Finally have each team member come and plot their emotional state onto the timeline. This works best done all together in a group as people feel less self-conscious that way. Get each person to draw a continuous line from the start of the timeline to the end. When the line is above the horizontal axis this indicates positive feelings, below the line being negative. Use different coloured pens to distinguish the lines clearly.

The team can then discuss their observations of the timeline, noting any discrepancies and identifying things to change based on the historical events and emotional states.

As an extension of this, try adding annotations to the lines describing the peaks and troughs, and specific feelings such as pride, frustration and boredom.

REVIEW PROJECTS WITH A LARGER GROUP

Many teams operate inside a larger ecosystem. They might work alongside ten other teams in a large organisation or alongside marketing and sales in a small start-up. Those teams that only run team-level retrospectives are in danger of locally optimising and missing out on a wealth of improvement opportunities.

Unfortunately, for many organisations, larger projects are still fraught with recurring problems and worse, recurring problems of the same nature. In short, many organisations still suck at projects even though there is plenty of opportunity to learn from our mistakes. So what's up? Why are we not learning? Why is there is a repetitive cycle that we just can't seem to break?

In addition, at the end of a project it is still common for teams to be disbanded and new teams to be formed with different people. On splitting up, those teams lose the momentum they have built up through working together. In his short paper *Developmental Sequence in Small Groups*, Bruce Tuckman describes the value of this momentum as the 'forming, storming, norming and performing' path, which describes how we learn to work with one another. Look to retain the learning and momentum by reviewing the project with everyone involved, beyond just a single team. By making the knowledge concrete, it can then be taken forwards and applied to the next project. Knowledge can also be turned from tacit to explicit in the form of changed organisational practices and principles.

Key benefits

Team-level retrospectives tend just to focus on the team and possibly those groups they regularly interact with. Progressive teams may extend their thinking towards the wider system, also improving other areas of the value stream they operate in.

Project-level retrospectives will open a whole new world of improvement opportunities. Involving all the parties required to deliver the project will focus the improvement on making the whole better, rather than potentially limiting the team to a local optimisation.

Punctuating the end of a project with an overall retrospective provides the opportunity to solidify learning that each person can then apply to the next project. It is, if you like, a live case study. This means that the learning gained from one project will start to permeate the whole organisation as people carry their acknowledged experience with them.

How to make it work

Given the larger scope of stakeholders involved in a project or programme, the larger overview session needs to be facilitated differently to a typical small team retrospective.

In order to make the most of the time available, particularly if the group is larger and some people are harder to get hold of, some upfront preparation is a good idea. We have had success from asking people to generate ideas before coming to the session. Asking them to email a list of subjects they would like to discuss, with a certain level of detail, is the simplest way of soliciting feedback. Alternatively you could use an online survey tool, which has the additional benefit that it is possible to give feedback anonymously. With the data gathered and distributed ahead of time, the session can become much more focused.

One question to answer is whether to distribute the consolidated feedback before the session. Sending it out ahead of time gets the creative juices flowing but take care in sensitive situations as not everyone is comfortable with criticism.

In a large forum, having each person check-in at the start of the session is even more important than it is at a regular team retrospective. As the number of attendees grows larger, the more likely it is that some person will be inhibited from giving potentially valuable views. A check-in for everybody will go some way to combat this problem. The check-in need not be a drawn-out affair, for example just a one-word description of how the project is going for them should help quite a bit. Alternatively take the opportunity to have some fun by describing progress as a film or car perhaps.

Your facilitator will earn their pay during this session, because larger retrospectives are hard work to facilitate. They will continually have to navigate the differing opinions, without taking sides, while all the time making sure that each voice gets a chance to be heard. They will need to keep the session focused on generating improvement ideas and learning, not dwelling on emotions or negative experiences too much. For this reason we suggest two things:

- Make this session longer than a normal team retrospective session. We suggest twice as long with a break.
- Have someone facilitate who has not been involved in the project to ensure impartiality.

As for getting people to come, we find making a business case does the trick. Take the time to describe the benefits to the organisation of doing the retrospective. Just putting these into money terms works wonders (never mind the intangible benefits). On large bodies of work this is as simple as saying, for example, 'If we could only get 1% better at our $30 million delivery, we would create $300,000 of value for the organisation'. It is usually hard for those busy people who might doubt the value of such a session to refuse a compelling economic statement.

COMPARE AGAINST MODELS, NOT TEAMS

As teams improve the way they work and the environment around them, it is natural that they will want to look at some yardstick for comparison. This could be to reassure them that they are headed in the right direction. Alternatively it could be to use as a data point to find gaps and weaker areas that could spur them to come up with valuable improvement ideas.

If team members only compare where they're at to where they were, they miss out on a much wider range of input and resources. Comparing their team to neighbouring teams in the organisation gives more diverse input, but without some common frame of reference, who is to say which team's practices are better? While getting input from other teams is great, copying their practices without understanding their context or the underlying principles that make them work will not necessarily yield the same results.

As a team, try measuring your maturity using a model in order to increase your awareness of principles and practices that could help you improve.

Key benefits

Periodically measuring maturity using a model gives regular and punctuated feedback on whether you are improving against the principles and values you give credence to. Models provide a reasonably objective, independent and reusable framework to measure against. Using a model forces the team to think beyond short-term problems towards a broader picture of how they operate and the progress they are making. The daily grind clouds a team's view. Taking the opportunity to look further and wider, and then seeing that they are actually making good progress can be very motivational.

How to make it work

When you are selecting a model be aware how important context is. Avoid blindly copying practices or taking absolutes from other contexts. Dan North presented an asymmetric function explaining the relationship of principles, practices and context at CukeUp 2015 in his talk 'you keep using that word'. He asserts that Practice = Principle(context), in other words, we shouldn't simply adopt the practices of others without considering the context within which they are applied.

One model we like is the *Seven pillars of agile* model developed by Brian Marick, Chet Hendrickson, Ron Jeffries, Bob Martin and James Shore. They identified seven pillars or abilities that are key to the success of agile teams. Underlying the pillars are some details on their nature, their importance and some points of evidence, which can be used as a set of criteria for meeting them.

The first time you run a retrospective comparing your team against a model, call out each attribute and describe its importance and its characteristics. Draw up a radar chart with a spoke and a scale (say 1-10) for each pillar. Then ask the team to consider its current level of maturity in each area. You could do this as a planning-poker consensus-based exercise, or get each individual to put their scores for each category on the chart. Provide time for team members to explain the reasons for their scores and in particular to discuss any significant discrepancies between their scores. Whichever way you run it, remember the scores are merely a guide to stimulate improvement ideas, so make sure that you don't waste time haggling over whether something is a three or a four on the scale. The score is specific to the team's context and largely irrelevant outside of the team.

Once the team has assessed their current maturity level, the next step is to reflect on and prioritise those areas the team thinks will benefit them the most. Then they should generate ideas for practices and processes in the top-priority area that would benefit the team and improve their capabilities to deliver.

The actions generated might not be easy to estimate or complete, for example, 'investigate a new practice or skill', so they may need some research, training, practice and further reflection. If so, great – these are opportunities for significant learning, whether you sustain the practice or not.

You could also get them to mark another set of values as an outline on the radar chart for where they would like to be in six months time, or maybe where their improvement actions might bring them to on the scale. This gives both a target to aim for and a yardstick against which to assess themselves later.

Teams we've worked with have found various models useful. The first model we used is the *XP Radar Chart*. The twelve principles of the *Agile Manifesto* make another good benchmark. For teams seeking feedback on their use of Scrum techniques and extending beyond it Henrik Kniberg's *Scrum Checklist* (not simply a checklist) is a good yardstick.

Progress against these frameworks doesn't happen overnight, so this is a type of retrospective that works well run periodically, maybe twice or three times a year.

DISSECT A STORY

Despite our good intentions and practice, some stories have a habit of blowing up in our faces. That 'simple five-point story' can turn into a sprint-spanning saga that makes Robert Jordan's 'Wheel of Time' books look like novellas (if you've read them you'll know what we mean, if not go and read them if you like fantasy and you have a few years to spare).

When user stories turn into epics and it's a long time before the team retrospects, the context and the degree of pain caused can be forgotten. Running a general retrospective with the usual wide remit and focus may mean people skirt around the edges of a problem story and don't get to the root of why it caused issues (or avoid discussing it altogether).

Instead of waiting for the next retrospective to roll round, take a problem story as soon as the team has finished with it and dissect it surgically. Scrutinise the delivery of the story to learn as much as possible from the experience, with the intention of improving future deliveries of this type of story or technology. Learn how to avoid repeating the same mistakes in future.

Key benefits

Dissecting a problematic story shortly after its completion allows the team members to inspect their decision-making and delivery approach, to help to avoid similar problems in the future.

Reviewing stories immediately after implementation provides fast, direct feedback. This is because the events are still fresh in the minds of the people involved. Focusing on the work rather than any individual contribution or performance makes discussion more objective and factual, removing some of the potential for emotions to obscure the lessons to be learned.

Specific questions allow the team to reflect on whether they just missed something this time or whether there are more systemic weaknesses that need to be addressed. When people are enmeshed in a problematic delivery they are often simply not aware of what needs improving. An objective inspection of a story using hard data prompts people to lift their heads and allows more independent and removed thinking.

The lessons learnt from this dissection can be used to improve the team's ways of working. The resulting improvement actions can be used to challenge whether current ways of working give a strong enough focus and discipline on the right practices and behaviours. This helps develop triggers to recognise warning signs and adjust decision making in future.

How to make it work

Start by holding the retrospective as close to the completion of the piece of work as possible. Plot the life of the story out sequentially, noting all the events, decisions, discoveries and interactions involved in getting the story to 'done'. If you use tasks, line them up chronologically and note who was involved. Supplement this timeline with any other events that occurred during the period. Capture all significant events, even if they might seem unrelated – further insights may show them as indirectly impacting delivery of the story. Consider using supplementary data about the story too, such as emails, test and build results, defects or even an area of design or code to add further detail to the timeline.

Once the team members organise the information, start to interrogate the story from different angles. The objective is to analyse the challenges faced, the options available, the decisions made and to reflect on how to improve in future. Think about different attributes of the delivery (for example speed, quality, predictability, technical debt) and ask specific questions to drive improvement ideas. Then consider the trade-offs in the decisions you make, such as doing more design at the outset maybe giving less variation in delivery timelines but slower feedback, versus emergent design potentially giving less redundancy and faster feedback but requiring more change later on. Focus on how the team can become better at managing these trade-offs.

For stories that took longer than expected, ask 'could it have been split, was it too big?' These answers could point toward a number of improvement ideas, such as spending more time refining the backlog or maybe some story-splitting education for the team. Check for unexpected work by asking 'Were there any tasks we did that we did not originally plan for?' If this is the case, it could point to a lack of time spent planning and designing or it might be work of an R&D nature that needs better communication about purpose and timelines. For acceptance problems, ask 'Did we miss anything?' (for example, backlog refinement, upfront acceptance criteria and tests, early enough feedback, early enough demo). If this is the case then review whether you had sufficient subject-matter expertise and stakeholder engagement when you needed it.

There are many other areas and questions you might like to explore, such as:

- Did we identify and manage all the dependencies adequately?
- Did we spot the risks and uncertainties and tackle them early enough – should we even have played the story at that point in time?
- Could we have predicted any of the things that blew up on us?
- Should we have spent more time learning about the story?
- Did we undertake any tasks that ended up not being needed, or were regretted because they incurred technical debt or rework or were performed out of sequence?
- Did we make good or bad choices (design, testing, release approach)?

Once you have answered these questions, consider what practices and ways of working will improve the situation and what behaviours to guard against.

RUN PERIODIC COMPLEXITY RETROSPECTIVES

As products grow, their degree of complexity nearly always increases, as more hands are involved in developing and maintaining them and more and more features are added. This complexity becomes a long-term-cost-of-ownership headache, as the product becomes harder and more costly to change over time.

Complexity can be hard to notice as it emerges, and it can creep into many areas of product development. The product may become too outwardly complex, unintuitive to use, bloated with rarely used features, under-perform or behave inconsistently. The product may also become inwardly complex, in the size of the code base, the cyclomatic complexity of its methods, the tests exercised against it, its resilience or how easy it is to support and diagnose issues. The design can suffer in such aspects as the interfaces and coupling of components, the drift of functional purpose, the clarity of domain or data model. There are other axes of complexity to consider too: the processes involved, the relationships between people and teams, geography and even the political and economic environment surrounding teams. There is a lot of potential for complexity that affects both products and teams.

Retrospectives may pick up on areas of complexity indirectly, voiced as complaints about areas of the code, design or testing. But complexity is rarely driven out as the root cause and is seldom the specific focus of retrospectives. This means that actions taken can be superficial, to alleviate short-term pain. They plaster over the cracks, rather than address the root cause.

Don't let complexity build up unchecked. In much the same way as our children grow tall in front of our eyes, complexity gradually builds up over time and can be best seen when compared to a former, simpler state. Run a retrospective that focuses on complexity. Identify many different areas of complexity and assess the level of complexity of the various aspects, then decide whether it is acceptable or whether action is required.

Key benefits

Teams who always optimise for delivering value as fast as possible may not appreciate the long-term implications of their decisions. This may result in a product that is hard to support, extend and maintain. Retrospecting on complexity provides the opportunity to explore whether the product will be supportable over the longer haul. This will help reduce the long-term cost of ownership of the product.

Focusing on complexity periodically will help to prevent a complex issue presenting itself at a very inconvenient point in time or when it is going to be much harder to resolve.

A retrospective that focuses on complexity will help people become more aware of its various forms and its detrimental impact. This awareness will help team members avoid introducing complexity in the future.

How to make it work

Start by agreeing the various types of complexity that you want to retrospect on. Our preference is to mix up a few different types of complexity to open thinking beyond just the code or design, which developers quickly tend to centre on. Here are some different types of complexity that we've seen used before, with some example criteria for each:

- *Internal to the product:* code, design, domain model, tests
- *The external product:* usability, consistency, feature usage
- *Delivering the product:* build and deploy pipeline, release process, configuration management
- *Supporting and maintaining the product:* monitoring and observability, analysing errors
- *Communication:* inter-team, stakeholders, media
- *Process and getting things done:* impediments, waste, bureaucracy

Once you've agreed the types of complexity you want to consider, assess the level of complexity that exists today. This works well as a radar chart, so take a whiteboard and draw a spoke for each criterion and give it a scale, from one to ten, with one being as simple as possible and ten being far too complex. Then have everyone think about the complexity in each area and jot down a number and some supporting reasons. Once everyone has noted down numbers and reasons for each

area, ask people to come up and mark their numbers on the board. We like to do this one spoke at a time, varying who goes first. To speed things up, you can give each person a different colour marker and have everyone do write at the same time.

When you have each person's score against a spoke, discuss the reasons for the values, focusing particularly on the outlying scores. Then agree on a value or take the average and move on. The scoring isn't as important as the discussion and resulting actions, so don't get stuck arguing between a six and a seven. It is a qualitative judgement and the relative complexity between criteria is more important than an absolute number. Connect the dots of each spoke to form a radar chart or spider web. With the most complex score of ten being on the outer edge of each spoke, the visual shape of the web will immediately strike the team with a clear view of where the most complexity is. The aim of the team is to keep the area of the web as small as possible. This retrospective is worth running periodically, to compare one radar chart to the next to show progress towards removing complexity over time.

While team members are deciding on a score for each spoke, they should write down the reasons behind their choices. Add these cards to annotate the diagram and use them to drive discussion towards courses of action. A good way to prompt action is to pick a spoke and work through the reasons for the complexity, noting down ways of reducing it. Ask what makes it complex? Why it has become that way? What is the impact of the complexity? Add a rough cost to implement or at least experiment with chosen reduction ideas, along with an expected impact and measure, then feed that into the work prioritisation process.

CONSIDER WASTE IN THE WIDER SYSTEM

Ask a team if they are as productive as possible and you will like get the unanimous answer 'Yes'. However ask a team member if the system is as productive as possible and you will get a very different answer.

Considering only personal team member productivity is a fundamental problem when retrospecting as a team. Team members may only consider themselves or maybe the team when they ask themselves how they could get better or more efficient. Only having a local point of view means team members will only have considered a tiny part of a huge puzzle.

If the team are not reminded of their place in a bigger system and the chance they have to go ahead and challenge things, teams will likely fall into the common trap which is 'it's always been done that way'. The waste will remain conveniently outside of their control.

Drive your retrospective from the lean principle 'remove waste'. Ask the team to identify all the waste they see. Ask them to consider not only waste that a person or team experiences but the waste in the larger system. Have them spend five minutes jotting down on post-it notes all those things they see as wasteful.

Key benefits

Most systems are hugely wasteful. In their book *Scaling Lean and Agile Development* Larman and Vodde say that in their experience 93% or more of product development time is waste. That number in itself should be encouraging, there is conservatively 90% of the system that surrounds you that you can improve. By choosing to use this perspective, the team will find many more areas for improvement.

Once people manage to shift their mindset from their waste to the waste of the system, they realise, as Keanu Reeves did in The Matrix, there is no spoon, the world is theirs and they are able to pick bullets out the air. If 90% of our system is waste, if we could remove just half of that waste we would be producing roughly five times more product, enough to conquer any industry that relies on technology. A caution though, in *User Story Mapping* Jeff Patton warns 'Building software faster is always a good idea. But it's never the solution'.

Another result of this shift in thinking is that it helps to achieve a greater perspective on the system as a whole. This change in perspective will shift teams away from optimizing locally to improving the wider world that they operate within. This will lead to the situation where teams will spot and remove waste that doesn't even affect them but that helps the wider system.

How to make it work

In a similar way to how we prioritised waste using the waste bin in *Visualise waste*, mark up a horizontal and ventical axis. Show the cost to remove the waste on the horizontal axis. Use the vertical axis for the impact of the waste. Ask team members to place each waste against the 2 axes. Remove the duplicate wastes as you go along to provide more clarity.

People will often disagree about the size and cost of wastes. Promote discussion about their difference in understanding. Explore the difference and add some clarifying text to the sticky notes. Do not spend a long time discussing the relative position of wastes. Positioning the wastes on the two axes is a fast method

of prioritisation and many of the lower priority wastes will not make it to the next stage of discussion.

After the team places all the waste ideas on the axes, they will be able to identify the low hanging fruit that sit in the top left hand corner (high impact, low cost of removal). Run through only the wastes in the top left hand corner and sort them into priority order relative to each other. Try adding an explicit cost of removal and impact to the wastes to help with prioritisation.

As the team members start to remove some of the biggest wastes in their immediate control, challenge them to expand their sphere of influence. Specifically, take a look at the things that are in the top right hand corner (high impact, high cost of removal) and articulate why these cost a lot to remove. Ask them to consider the cost for someone else to remove them. When they consider that it could be a senior member of the organisation who is removing the waste they

often reduce the cost estimate considerably. The cost to the team is reduced because it is an estimate of the effort to lobby a senior person to remove the waste. In addition, the senior person is likely to be much better equipped to navigate the organisation and remove the waste than the team members themselves. The cost of lobbying will often be very low, as it can be as simple as making the cost of the problem and recommended fix explicitly clear to 'the people who can'.

We've seen some great outcomes from involving management in unblocking problems, particularly those that span the organisation. Firstly they are very good at traversing and influencing parts of the company, they probably learnt that on their travels through to management. Secondly it provides a connection and opportunity for that manager to go to *gemba* and go and see the work, understand the problems first hand so they can help unblock and empower the team to solve some of them for themselves.

ADAPTING THE ENVIRONMENT

GET A ROOM

The prime directive for retrospectives described by Norman Kerth in his book *Project Retrospectives: A Handbook for Team Reviews* emphasises the key point that safety is paramount for success. Airing your dirty laundry in public is never easy, so the degree of safety a team feels is directly affected by the environment they conduct retrospectives in.

If the team thinks they are being judged by co-workers, or by those who might determine their pay, career progression and ultimately success, then they are not likely to feel safe. Under these circumstances any retrospective is likely to be superficial at best, pointless at worst.

For a team to truly improve, they need to show vulnerability, and to do this, they need to feel safe. Part of feeling safe is having privacy.

The easiest way of having privacy is to get a room. This may seem simple and obvious, but its effects are very powerful. The team needs to feel they can talk about absolutely anything, safe in the knowledge that 'it will go no further than these four walls'.

Key benefits

Getting a room for your retrospective session pays back dividends. It ensures that you are getting the most from your investment of time by encouraging open and honest dialogue about the things that matter, as opposed to ignoring the big issues.

Having a room will change the team's attitude to retrospectives. Not having the trappings of everyday working life in front of them emphasises the importance of the time spent in the room. Making the investment in the session by going to a room rather than just staying in the team space sets the tone for investment in continuous improvement itself.

A further significant benefit to getting a room is that it removes many other distractions that plague the modern workplace. Moving to a room reduces the amount of disruption from emails, any other kind of work or people approaching the team. One way you can further this is to agree to ban various items from the room such as phones, laptops etc.

How to make it work

If the team has a permanent room to themselves, then lucky them – most teams we have worked with don't. If not, then make sure to book a meeting room on a recurring basis.

When you are picking a room, choose what works best for the team. If they are not happy with the overhead of going upstairs to the meeting suite on the ninth floor, make sure that the booking is close to the team's work area. Alternatively, as mentioned in the section *Take it outside*, it may be desirable to get completely away from the workspace.

Make sure you can't be overheard or disturb anyone else, so you can laugh and let off steam without inhibiting the outcome of the retrospective. Ben worked with a team who wrote software for electronic trading systems. In a retrospective session, they had a colleague come looking for a member of the team because they needed them to answer a question to allow them to continue their work. The effect of that interruption, the removal of one of the team members and the subsequent break killed the retrospective. The team struggled to pick up where they left off. At the next retrospective, one of the team members came to the session with an immediate improvement idea. They suggested that they put a sign on the door 'Retrospective in Progress' in order that people looking for a member of their team realise that it is a meeting that they can't interrupt. The rest of the team immediately agreed with the proposal, adopting it into their ongoing way of working.

The layout of the room is important too. Ideally the room layout should be an open space with seats in a circle, as Esther Derby and Diana Larsen point out in *Agile Retrospectives: Making Good Teams Great*. It may seem superficial but the physical barrier that a table brings also introduces a psychological barrier between members of the team.

Don't skimp on space and whiteboards to display artefacts from the team and the mandatory sticky note invasion, but also to get creative, draw diagrams, pictures, grids, emotions ... whatever comes up! If this is not possible then try to get a room with enough flip charts. Though be warned – super sticky Post-it notes are easily rearranged on whiteboards, but it's much harder if you've stuck them on flip charts.

We worked in a building in London that had meeting rooms where two sides of each room were floor-to-ceiling windows. It was up a few floors, so a nice environment for retrospectives, just not very practical. In a retrospective that Ben was facilitating the team ran out of room on the whiteboards, but they simply kept going onto the windows. The point here is to adapt your environment to your needs or adapt your needs to your environment.

Other teams in the same building commandeered empty offices to hold their retrospectives. They felt that although the rooms were on the small side, it was a price worth paying for privacy.

Although it's very important that people can visualise the topics of conversation, it's also necessary to retain the level of safety built in to the retrospective. As with good test practice, we should tear down our retrospective environment, by removing all the information we put on the walls and disposing of it safely.

ADAPTING THE ENVIRONMENT

INVOLVE BUSINESS STAKEHOLDERS

Safety is important for retrospectives, which is why it's common to have only team members attend. Sometimes teams include one or more customer representatives, who would naturally attend too. But any project is bound to have business stakeholders or customers who are outside the team. If they are always excluded, then the team misses out on certain opportunities to improve.

So when should we invite them and when not? When there is an organisational problem? When there is a problem with the business stakeholder? When we've just had a good sprint and conversations will be positive? Should we always invite them? Never invite them?

The fact is that having a business stakeholder present is likely to inhibit a team in some way or another, at least while the relationship is new. This might manifest itself as mildly as a developer failing to mention an acceptance test that they left broken in order to come to the retrospective. At its most detrimental though, it can completely stifle any chance of improvement. Given that the main purpose of retrospectives is to surface major problems, the whole team needs to feel safe to do this without fear of bad outcomes. Having someone who could influence career progression present, but who isn't yet trusted, may well mean that any elephants in the room don't get unveiled.

If you don't invite business stakeholders to team retrospectives, you won't surface as many improvement ideas regarding relationships with them. What ideas you do come up with will require additional effort after the retrospective to get buy-in from the stakeholder. This is likely to be wasteful.

Teams who are not comfortable inviting their business stakeholders should look more deeply into why that is.

Maybe it's time to run an introspective retrospective session, although we don't fancy thinking of a chapter title for that one.

In short, there is definitely a time and place to invite your business stakeholders.

Key benefits

Unfortunately in many stakeholder-team relationships there are trust issues. Inviting a business stakeholder, even just from time to time, will do wonders to build the relationship, regardless of whether or not you choose to address the trust issue directly. We have seen some miraculous changes in behaviour from both team members and business stakeholders, just because the retrospective session has given them the opportunity to see things from the other's point of view. A business stakeholder who sees that team members care enough to try to improve their delivery and team members who hear the business stakeholder's troubles will align their objectives and work harder together.

Inviting the business stakeholders builds trust and understanding. The team members see the pressures that the business stakeholder is under to deliver their product and they in turn see that the retrospective is driving improvements and waste removal and isn't a hippy agile thing to let the team slack off.

Business stakeholders have a different perspective and influence within the organisation. When a stakeholder is present and offering to help, it can resolve problems that the team are struggling with. Finally, if the team feels they have a problem with their stakeholder relationship, they will only ever get to the root of the problem with stakeholders present.

How to make it work

Invite your business stakeholders along to a retrospective. Although this sounds simple we've seen stakeholders react weirdly because they don't understand the term 'retrospective'. Drop the 'retrospective' title and instead replace it with a title that your business stakeholder will respond positively to. Call it an 'Improvement' session or 'Get things done quicker' session.

The first time a team has a session with a business stakeholder, the members are often nervous. This is not surprising given interaction with the stakeholder usually involves some kind of judgement. Maintain the mantra 'we just want to get better' and if there are still objections then maybe it's time to go and work somewhere that values continuous improvement.

Try having a specific theme for the first few times the business stakeholder attends. Doing this will likely keep the session on topic, which will be safer if there are any reservations about airing dirty laundry. In addition, having a clear topic for improvement will encourage the business stakeholder to attend since they will have confidence that it will be time well spent.

It is a good idea to spend some time to prime your business stakeholders in advance, to encourage them not to shut down ideas and topics in the retrospective and be open to hearing some of the bad things about the organisation without wincing or getting defensive, as that will put the barriers up.

Do not however invite your stakeholders to all of your retrospectives. For the same reason that teams choose to go to a room for safety, inviting the business stakeholder to all sessions could potentially inhibit honest retrospection.

There is no exact formula here, just be aware of the benefits and impact of having stakeholders present.

THROW FOOD INTO THE MIX

with. Because of that, it's a good idea to occasionally provide a snack along with a retrospective session.

You have probably noticed that food provides people with a shared point of focus, often serving as an icebreaker in its own right. Next time you are at a party, stand near the buffet and you'll be amazed at how easily the conversations start. People say the Brits love talking about the weather but we suspect they love talking about whatever it is that distracts them from their social inadequacies. Having food at a retrospective provides the perfect icebreaker for attendees and it should come as no surprise that food attracts attention even from the most reluctant team member.

A simple and effective trick to increase participation during busy periods is to take people out for lunch, or bring food into the meeting room and invite team members to take a quick bite and discuss the team's processes.

Key benefits

If the team has been having a hard time of late and you introduce food, you will lighten the mood. There is something about having food in the room that encourages people to have fun.

Having food at a retrospective session is a cheap way of making it a positive experience and ensuring that participants are eager to attend next time.

If it's an unexpected treat for the team, having some food provides a small reward or says 'well done'. As

Teams are always busy. There is always more demand for their time than there is time to give. This makes it hard to tempt them away from the hustle and bustle of delivery in order to retrospect. Even the most creative and energising of facilitators sometimes struggles to peel teams away from their desks.

Retrospectives can also be heated affairs, where passionate feelings about how to improve come out and differences of opinion are aired. However, it is hard to stay angry with someone that you have broken bread well as you basking in the knowledge that you have made someone else's day a little bit brighter, it has also been proven that small rewards like these improve motivation amongst team members.

Archaeologists have identified evidence for shared meals dating back to the Paleolithic era, when our Homo Sapiens ancestors first emerged. The thinking here is that there is a long history of bonding and reconciling differences over food.

How to make it work

🔧 Food can be a sensitive subject for some so try to make sure that all people are considered. Please don't go out and just buy doughnuts if you know someone on the team is trying to eat healthily, as this won't help them reach their goal and will pressure them to eat to conform. We definitely don't want that.

Having said that, we have worked with many teams that were all happy to tuck into the sugary ring-shaped treats. After a while though, the box of doughnuts seemed less of a treat. Interestingly, it was only doughnuts that faded in popularity and not the use of food. Instead the teams started to buy savoury snacks and fruit. Even a cheese board made it to the table once (beware strong cheeses and small rooms).

Consider that not everyone wants to share from the same plate. Some people like tearing off a chunk of pizza but consider those who don't. If you think that someone might be sensitive to sharing from the same plate it's worth having an option where they can open a sealed packet. At the least, consider informal team rules like no double dipping.

Bringing food to the table is a responsibility that might start to feel like a burden. To avoid that happening, ensure that the team has a clear and transparent system for choosing the person responsible for this task.

Years ago, we both worked on a team that decided to implement a system we called piggy points (we have since seen it called numpty points too). We are not quite sure how the piggy points name came about. They were doing Scrum at the time so maybe it was an extension of the famous 'chicken and pig' fable but its root seems to have been lost in the mists of time. This system was something that the team had decided on as part of their way of working. They decided to penalise each team member or Scrum master with one piggy point when they were late to stand up. At the end of the sprint, before the retrospective session, the team then counted up the piggy points awarded and the person who had the highest tally had the dubious honour of going out and buying the treats. Oink Oink.

This nice bit of fun works to incentivise this team to turn up to stand up on time. Here are some other simple systems we have come across:

- Potluck arrangement where everyone brings something
- Rotating responsibility, where the purchaser chooses the treat
- Management contribution
- Stakeholder gift

CHOOSE TO TRAVEL

A retrospective is, amongst other things, a chance to inspect and adapt the team's way of working in a safe environment. Although it is generally appreciated that co-located teams perform better, many large organisations still group geographically dispersed people into a single team. Even when all of the members of a team are co-located it is often the case that other teams they work closely with are not. It is certainly common to see organisations where stakeholders such as the product management group are not co-located.

This becomes a problem for a number of reasons. Firstly, consider the behaviour of many car drivers when they are involved in an incident with another vehicle on the road. They are quick to lose their temper, safe in the knowledge that they are separated from the other driver by the steel box they sit in. In this situation people often behave in a very different manner than if they were two people walking along the street. Whilst we hope that in your work environment there are no negative hand gestures in the (webcam) mirror, we have observed some more passive and less confrontational versions of these reactions between team members that do not physically meet often.

In addition, mutual care and respect is increased when people have met one another and they get to know each other. Physical presence allows non-verbal communication and helps team members to build rapport effectively.

When working with geographically dispersed teams, try to organise retrospectives where everyone is physically present regularly. The ideas generated will

tend to be beneficial to the wider team, not just to the people based in one location. Equally, the payback will be far greater than just the improvement ideas. Relationships, empathy with other team members and motivation may all receive a boost.

Key benefits

Bringing the wider team together for face-to-face communication fosters stronger and more rapid team-building and collaboration than alternatives such as the telephone or telepresence. It also helps team members to identify with one another as individuals.

Face-to-face retrospection refreshes respect for team members by allowing them to get things off their chests. Often these are things that they do not feel comfortable talking about over the telephone.

Once the team members have built bonds by doing a retrospective face-to-face, subsequent remote work is likely to be much more effective and collaborative. Team members will be much less likely to just send an email, instead opting to open a chat channel, pick up the phone or set up a video call.

Finally team members who have met but usually work in different time zones are much more likely to try to resolve problems before their counterparts are expected into the office or after they have left.

If the teams have agreed a shared responsibility, face-to-face, they are much more likely to abide by such an agreement than if it was handed to them or agreed over email. For example we have seen the level of responsibility taken for global build monitors increase significantly following a face-to-face retrospective.

How to make it work

Unfortunately travel, particularly long-distance, is expensive, for it to be viewed as worthwhile we need to demonstrate its value. You could use the idea *Create a business case* for this, but you will still have to demonstrate the return for stakeholders. Make the assumptions behind the business case visible, such as a projected increase in productivity from solving joint problems or lower cost of ownership from shared understanding and collective ownership. However for your first face-to-face get-together, these assumptions are likely to be strongly challenged because there won't be a precedent or comparison and no feedback on the positive effects. In addition it is very hard to place a cost on not doing a face-to-face retrospective.

To make a more compelling case, combine the retrospective with other activities that would benefit from face-to-face interaction. For example, expand the trip to include product or technical design sessions, to work in cross-team pairs, or to share knowledge. Making the retrospective coincide with the delivery of a business or project milestone also boosts the case for travel and has the added benefit of allowing teams to plan the next milestone while together.

Once you've convinced stakeholders that travel is a sensible investment, make sure that you record the outputs, improvements and increases in your way of working in a tangible way, even if the measures are qualitative. This ammunition will make your next request for money to travel much less strenuous.

If you don't have the opportunity to travel often, chose a retrospective technique that allows you to retrospect on a longer timeframe. The ideas *Use timelines with different dimensions* and *Review projects with a larger group* give good examples of retrospective formats for this. In addition, set aside more time than you would for a team whose members regularly see each other. We recommend allowing from two hours to a day when doing a larger retrospective between teams that are geographically dispersed.

TAKE IT OUTSIDE

Repeating the same retrospective in the same space can become mundane. We've certainly been there. Watching people staring at their phones for the answers to life, the universe and everything can be frustrating for team members who've turned up eager to discuss exciting improvement ideas.

If teams go to the same room for every retrospective and stare at (or climb) the same four walls, with the same people and the same facilitator, they are very likely to approach the same problems in the same way, not to mention getting bored. Brains will switch off – after all, they know how the last similar retrospective ended, so they will expect this session to end the same way. Things will grow stale and the team will struggle to generate new insights. As result the motivation for continuous improvement will lessen too.

We advocate getting a room for retrospectives to provide safety and enable openness. If however, the room is round the corner from where the team usually work or even on the same floor, people will inevitably get disturbed from time to time. Even just turning the interrupters away can disrupt the flow and potentially stop something sensitive but important being said. Team members are more likely to pop out and grab coffee or just check something and before you know it, a whole load of time is lost, or possibly the creation of a profound insight.

Without leaving the box, you are unlikely to be able to think outside the box, so move around and go to an unfamiliar environment. Ideally leave the building, or if that's too much, then at least go to another floor. Go somewhere new.

Key benefits

Just having a break from the norm will re-establish the team members' level of participation, will shift their thinking out of the confines of work and visibly lift them. We bet you'll get a much better attendance when you schedule the retrospective outside the office. Think of it as a mini team-building exercise, a way to strengthen the team.

Moving to an unfamiliar environment causes something magical to happen. Those people who were once half-asleep on an autopilot of repetition will be awake and aware of their surroundings and more aware of the problems that they are trying to solve.

Tom remembers an example where the leadership team of his company were taken out of the office to the London Olympic site, as it was being built, to meet a local fencing team, Newham Swords, who were being coached by Olympic fencers. The coaches gave the team members fencing tuition, to help them learn how to give and receive feedback and how to teach each other. The inspiration of being in a completely different context, watching the dramatic benefit of combining coaching and practice, led to an agreement to move learning and development away from classroom certification courses towards practice and mentorship-driven learning, a huge shift in mentality.

The act of leaving the building punctuates your retrospective as an important event. Investing the effort to do this is a clear statement of the value you place in the output of the retrospective.

How to make it work

Taking your retrospective somewhere new doesn't necessarily require you to book ahead or plan far in advance or even cost any money. It doesn't even need to take too much thought. Leaving the building and going to find some open space is well worth the investment in time. Going to a park and sitting on the grass or any space where you can be comfortable and hear each other is enough to stimulate the mind into thinking differently.

We have seen some excellent results from just leaving the building and going to some open uncrowded space. Ben was visiting a financial institution in the United States. He spoke to a couple of members of a leadership team who each separately told him how they had a really good level-setting session the previous day. The head of the leadership team had taken it outside. On a beautiful spring day in Jersey City and at a moment's notice, he had taken his leadership team out of the rather subdued office and down to the Hudson River. He had then continued to run his retrospective in much the same manner that he had in the past but with a hugely different result.

When you hold a retrospective session outside, you will have to use a rather different format for the discussions. People are not likely to have the output from the last iteration handy, and they are not likely to be putting sticky notes up and dot voting. This format is much more suited to blowing away the cobwebs, surfacing team feelings and not feeling bound by having to produce a concrete list of improvement actions.

DO REMOTE RETROSPECTIVES

Although in *Choose to travel* we said that it is important to meet people face to face, the reality is that this cannot always happen in global organisations. The quality of a retrospective is reduced when it is not conducted face to face. However it is still better to have a retrospective than none at all.

Arranging and running a remote retrospective session is harder work than the equivalent face-to-face session. It requires you to navigate room availability in different locations. The preferred rooms will probably be highly utilised because of their video conferencing capabilities. Then you have to consider how to run a retrospective over video conferencing, making sure that everyone gets airtime and can see and hear each other. To further complicate matters, there are often more participants than just a single team of five to seven people. All this can put people off running remote retrospectives

altogether. But for teams and stakeholders split across multiple sites this is the only possible way they can retrospect on their way of working. If it's not done, a huge opportunity is lost at the project level.

Distributed teams that miss the opportunity to communicate suffer the negative effects of Conway's law. In *How Do Committees Invent*, Melvin Coway wrote that 'organizations which design systems ... are constrained to produce designs which are copies of the communication structures of these organizations'. As a result it should come as no surprise when the various components of their products also don't communicate effectively. This leaves both the organisations and software systems fragmented.

Take the time to do cross-location retrospectives, using the highest bandwidth communications available.

Key benefits

As a cheaper alternative to travelling, a cross-location retrospective using high bandwidth communications like video-conferencing is a good opportunity to re-establish a way of working for a project consisting of distributed teams and stakeholders.

Where the delivery teams are on one site and the stakeholders are on another, doing remote retrospectives can be incredibly rewarding as it will really help increase the level of trust between the two parties. It is not common to experience high levels of trust built purely over formal meetings on the phone.

Even if the size and nature of a remote retrospective can inhibit deep retrospection and compelling actions, they can still be valuable as an expectation setting session. Openly sharing experience and perspective can be enlightening for the whole group.

How to make it work

Preparation is key to the success of running remote retrospectives. You will need to consider facilitation, required outcome, visualisation, format and materials.

You should aim for a facilitator in each location. This helps if you need to run activities locally, such as diverge and merge. Agree responsibilities between regional facilitators. It is important that you have a clear understanding of who is running the session. Have a chief facilitator whom others yield to. In a larger session you might suffer from having people talk over one another, promoted by even the smallest lag in audio between locations. Make sure that the facilitators lead by example.

Make the purpose of the session very clear in an agenda and circulate this ahead of time. Having people's expectations aligned beforehand will save a lot of time spent at the start of the session getting people on the same page.

Make sure that your visualisations are appropriate for your room set-up. Remember do not use walls that cannot be seen by the camera and write using large block capitals to make it clearer for remote participants to read the detail themselves.

Gather data beforehand. Use the remote session to prioritise topics by voting on them and discuss each using firm time-boxes. We describe a few ways of doing this in *Review projects with a larger group*.

Make sure that you have the required material in each location. If people will be expected to review materials or write sticky notes then make sure that your local facilitator provides them.

In order that you get the most out of your session, ensure that you have the highest bandwidth communications available to you. For larger groups a telephone is not enough. Running remote sessions works well in specific telepresence rooms or failing that in meeting rooms with video conferencing. High bandwidth communication is very important. It helps avoid communication issues such as people talking over one another and possibly inflaming a situation rather than improving it. Get people to talk more slowly than usual and to be very aware that they are not just interacting with people in the room and encourage them to face the camera when providing their insight. Finally, don't be that person at the movies rustling their snack-wrapper – the sound is disproportionately amplified up by many microphones.

DIM THE LIGHTS

Bill Watterson, the author of the comic strip Calvin and Hobbes, wrote: 'You can't just turn on creativity like a faucet. You have to be in the right mood'. While he may have gone on to joke that only last-minute panic is the right mood, there is no easy way to approach a session that requires creative thinking. Asking people to apply De Bono's *Six Thinking Hats* and metaphorically put on the green hat of creativity might provide some mental space to be creative, but it doesn't guarantee that creativity will follow.

When you need to stimulate creativity, try dimming the lights. We came upon this idea when researching possible ways to drive out more radical and creative thinking, and have found it is an effective way of getting people to come up with creative ideas. Anna Steidle and Lioba Werth, in *Freedom from constraints: Darkness and dim illumination promote creativity*, explain that people assess their physical environment immediately after entering a room, and behave appropriately. In general, rooms with lower lighting levels promote a safer environment and as a result more adventurous behaviour. This adventurous behaviour leads to more creative ideas.

Key benefits

Dimmed lights promote a feeling of freedom from constraints which in turn helps creative thinking. When the lights are dimmed, people tend to down-play the often self-imposed constraints of working in an office environment, and they tend to become less risk-averse. This is most important during idea generation, because, it promotes more radical solutions. Dimming the lights in your retrospective room can be an extremely quick and cost-effective way of stimulating creative thinking.

How to make it work

There are two predominant lighting environments you might start from, each requiring a different approach to getting the right level of light in the meeting room.

If the room has no natural light, you need to add a source of light. Normally when people use a space like this, they would just switch on the (probably fluorescent) lighting. If the room has dimmer switches, it is very easy for you to adjust the lighting levels down a notch or two from usual. Unfortunately, most offices do not have dimmer switches. We have found that battery-powered camping lamps are a perfect solution. They are relatively cheap and often adjustable.

The other case is where the room has an abundance of natural light. In this case, blinds, curtains and screens will all help you achieve the desired level of lighting. If your usual room does not have blinds, it could take quite a lot of persuasion to get blinds installed, probably more than just pointing to scientific research. As a faster alternative, find another room where you can control the levels of light to better suit your needs. If you would benefit from keeping your usual space and there aren't any blinds, use another reason to petition for them. We worked with a team who found it a happy coincidence that they also needed to restrict the amount of light in order to work with a projector. This reasoning was much more palatable to those who controlled the budgets when the team asked for funding for blinds.

While reducing lighting levels helps promote creativity, reducing lighting levels too far is counter-productive. If the team members can't see each other in the room, they will lose the benefits of non-verbal visual communication. If people struggle to read sticky notes, creativity levels will drop away. Aim to reduce lighting to a level noticeably below what would be normally expected, but still make it easy to see the rest of the room. In the first case this will be enough to promote an injection of energy and ultimately creativity into the room. Over time, play around with different lighting levels to find what works best with your teams.

You can also experiment with periods of dim lighting. Research suggests that dim lighting works best for the idea generation part of creative thinking, and that brighter lights are more stimulating for evaluating those ideas. However, we have had success running whole retrospectives with dimmer lighting. Try reducing the lighting at certain points to help with idea generation, for example during brainstorming time.

If you decide to use intermittent dimming, the level to which you dim the lights can be much more extreme. Try leaving just enough light for team members to see the page in front of them but not everything around the room. This will have the nice side-effect that it will focus concentration on the task at hand, and any mobile phones lighting up will be immediately obvious to everyone in the room.

FACILITATING SESSIONS

DON'T JUST SAY 'WE CAN'T'

A statement of fact such as 'we can't do it' tends to close down any further conversation. Good facilitators need to spot such situations and rescue the discussion. Often, the person making this statement did not deliberately mean to derail a meeting, but has said it for one of two reasons:

- They are limited by their experience and knowledge.
- They might have made a judgement in their mind that the cost benefit analysis is not favourable.

In both cases, the outcome is verbalised as 'we can't'.

With infinite resources anything is possible. If we had access to the brightest minds in the world and enough time, we could achieve anything. Saying 'we can't' and having unlimited resources are two extreme ends of the spectrum and things are not usually binary if we stop to consider them in more depth.

To exacerbate the problem, the other team members rarely argue against such a statement. This is because the person most likely to have an opinion on the feasibility of an idea is the most experienced one. Alternatively, the most dominant person in a team often makes such strong statements. In both cases, the others will be discouraged from challenging their judgement.

The outcome is that teams just dismiss some solutions out of hand without discussing their underlying assumptions, and ultimately miss out on potential improvements. So instead of just saying 'we can't', spend some time exploring the underlying reasons. The results can be very revealing!

Explore the reasons for the initial reaction. Challenge the underlying, unspoken, assumptions. Quite often we find that teams unearth one or two of these underlying assumptions that they fundamentally disagree on.

Key benefits

Refusing to stop at 'we can't' means we don't prematurely rule potential improvements out due to false or unexplored assumptions and miss out on opportunities to explore improvement ideas.

Also significant is that asking 'why' helps the team to think of more possibilities and start to think more factually about what is involved in decision-making and what makes an idea a good investment of time (effort) and money. This will make them more capable of independent decision-making and problem-solving.

It also spreads knowledge across the team of the pros and cons of possible improvement ideas, bringing team alignment and hopefully autonomy.

Lastly we have applied collective reasoning: we have used the creativity and experience of the collective team to refine an improvement idea. This in itself improves the way the team functions.

How to make it work

Find some way of not allowing 'we can't' to be a satisfactory final statement. A retrospective facilitator such as a scrum master can specifically look out for these 'statements of fact', but a better idea is to make it one of your team principles not to use the phrase 'we can't'.

It is quite often handy to ask these questions:

* With infinite time and money, would the response still be 'we can't'?
* Ask 'based on what?'
* Repeatedly ask 'why?'

As a start, imagine that you had infinite time and money – would the answer still be the same? We've found that posing the infinite resource question leads people to unravel the inbuilt assumptions about what makes the proposal difficult.

Another way to open up this dialogue is to ask 'based on what?' This question makes people analyse their thoughts, and hopefully challenge some of their own assumptions. Get team members to present their assumptions to the rest of the team, put them up on a board, prioritise them and then discuss whether they're valid and what the cost of changing them might be.

A third useful question is 'why'. Its use, increasingly popular in software delivery circles, is described by Taiichi Ohno in *Toyota Production System: Beyond Large-Scale Production*. Toyota used a succession of 'whys' to drill down to the root cause when they were trying to solve problems. They found that five whys were probably sufficient to drive out the true root cause rather than the immediately obvious but possible superficial cause. We can apply a similar technique, one often used by children to annoy their parents when they tell them 'no'. Keep asking 'why' until we flush out all the real reasons why people think that something is going to be difficult or impossible.

Funnily enough, it turns out that experts are human after all. They are constrained by their past experiences, not just the technology or domain, but also their past successes and failures. After exploring assumptions thoroughly, sometimes you hear something like 'I don't know, it's just always been that way', which is a red flag for a 'please challenge me' question. Remember, their reasons for rejecting something based on previous experience may no longer be valid, as technology and the tools are changing all the time.

DON'T LET FACILITATORS SOLVE PROBLEMS

Whether it is right or wrong, it is a matter of fact, most facilitators have been team managers at some point or another. Moreover a manager whose primary responsibility was solving problems for those she managed. This is a hard dynamic for many facilitators who might deny they ever solve problems but then eventually fess up.

Most managers care passionately about the teams they work with and can often see a way to resolve the team's immediate problems. So they think it helpful to step in and suggest a solution for the team to execute, or worse, take the responsibility for fixing the team's problem themselves.

The drawback is that although it is tempting for the facilitator to fix the problems and in the short term, seemingly more efficient, in the longer term, the facilitator is actually denying the team the opportunity to develop the skills to solve problems for themselves. 'Hold on, my scrum master's job is to remove impediments to the team' I hear you say. However, this creates a dependency on the facilitator, which might well get stronger rather than weaker over time.

Try to work by the principle that everything facilitators do for a team should reduce the team's reliance on them a little or make their role a little more redundant (remember that when you make your role redundant you are more likely to get promoted than fired).

There are two recurring failure modes that we see in this situation and as facilitators we must avoid.

First, as facilitators, we must resist jumping in. We might think we are acting in the best interests of the team by coming up with a solution to a problem they have identified, but in reality we deny them the chance to solve the problem for themselves.

When a solution is described rather than a need, it is likely that any resulting outcome will be sub-optimal. Of the many reasons for this, not using all the skills and brain power of all the members of the retrospective is wasteful. Also there is a lack of ownership when a team are handed a solution rather than presented with a problem. The upshot is a team who might not appreciate why they are doing what they are doing while also missing out on an opportunity to improve their problem-solving skills.

The second, and arguably worse, failure mode is when the facilitator takes responsibility to fix the problem themselves. In this situation, a team identifies a problem in a retrospective which the facilitator steps in to take away and fix, because they know the systems, organisation, people or solutions of the past. In this case, we have many of the same problems as before but with the additional disadvantage that team members may not even know how the problem has been solved.

When the facilitator solves the problem, the next time the team face a similar problem, they will not know how to go about starting to rectify the situation. Instead, they will either have to find the facilitator or worse, wait until their next retrospective to raise this latest problem.

How to make it work

As a facilitator, back off. Even if you see an opportunity to solve a problem in a more efficient way, remember that is a short-term efficiency while the long-term efficiency of the team depends on the team learning how to fix problems themselves.

Make sure that the team knows the root cause of the problem. Techniques such as the '5 Whys' and *Ishikawa's fishbone model*, can help to discover that.

Use open questions in retrospectives to help the team drive their own solutions. Ask focusing questions like 'What possible courses of action do we have and which can you control or influence?' Write these suggestions down, even if they seem impossible, as the act of displaying them will likely prompt exploration of the underlying assumptions and further derivatives of the original idea.

Finally, no one likes to see people struggle with a problem at length. If you as a facilitator must offer your insight, first, ask permission. Once you have the agreement of the team tell the team explicitly that you are taking off your 'facilitator hat' and that you are contributing as a team member. Once you have presented your idea as an option, don your facilitator hat again without trying to influence the team further.

This doesn't mean letting the team drive off the cliff. You can always challenge, but remember, every time you step in as another time they might not in future!

Key benefits

This idea means playing the long game. Used successfully to remove the reliance on the facilitator, it will provide greater long-term speed and throughput for your team.

By developing the problem-solving techniques that teams naturally have and applying them to solving organisational problems, team members will become more empowered. They will feel more ownership of a solution to a problem if they have designed it. This ownership will translate to a greater success rate.

This empowerment will bring a shift of focus within teams to fixing problems rather than sitting on them waiting for help, or just working round them. This agitation will start to change the dynamic and culture within an organisation as problems become things to solve and not immovable obstacles.

STAND AND DELIVER

Running a retrospective session without enough energy in the room limits the amount of exploration and thought that goes into generating improvement ideas. This results in missed opportunities to push the boundaries of improvement. If the team members and facilitator are comfortable in their chairs then it is far easier for the retrospective to drift along without this much-needed energy. This comfort can also make it easier for the loudest voices to dominate proceedings, allowing others to switch off.

Stand-up meetings derived their name from their deliberate intention to solve the problem of lack of energy and momentum. Try to apply the same logic by running your retrospective with everyone standing up.

Key benefits

First and foremost, running a standing retrospective injects more energy. If people are on their feet, they are much less inclined to daydream, become distracted by their phones or fall asleep (or at least the penalty of falling asleep is high enough to deter people).

Quieter members of the team are more likely to engage and voice their opinions, because everyone automatically becomes an active participant when they are standing. Having all team members participate means that a wider range of problems and solution options are explored, rather than just those chosen by the more active or more vocal participants. As a result of the increased participation, the level of buy-in to an improvement action increases and everyone feels they own the solutions.

Using this format focuses attention on the outcome of the retrospective. No one likes to stand around for an hour or more with nothing to show for it, so people will focus better and think harder to get a result. A word of warning however: this increased focus on outcomes can lead to people taking shortcuts, for example, failing to challenge the thinking and assumptions behind improvement ideas. This tendency could mean ideas fail to deliver the best results, so watch out for that.

The increase in efficiency will probably lead to shorter retrospectives, having the lovely knock-on effect that people come already focused and positive about the session. If your ninety-minute retrospectives were valuable in what they achieved, halving the time and achieving the same output effectively doubles your return on time spent.

Doing a scheduled standing retrospective is a small step towards continuous retrospective and improvement. Creating quality results in less time through standing up in retrospectives can encourage a mentality of on-demand retrospection based on responses to events.

How to make it work

When you consider the room set-up, make sure there are no chairs or places to get too comfortable. This is not an absolute rule though. The balance you are trying to achieve is an environment where people are uncomfortable enough that they are focused on getting a successful outcome but not so uncomfortable that they vow never to attend another retrospective.

So, can we use stools? How about perching on the edge of a desk, does that count as not standing? It's up to you. Remove what seems appropriate as it may not be practical to remove all objects that could be commandeered for sitting on. We have had successful sessions where people have perched on a table left in the room. The key point is that the barrier to getting involved is much lower than if people were sitting on chairs, legs firmly positioned under the table, or a long way from the whiteboard, flip chart or other materials

in use. When we started using this approach, it turned out that this was often all that was needed to get much greater participation in retrospectives.

Move chairs and other obstacles outside for an hour, remembering Grace Hopper's immortal advice, 'it's easier to ask forgiveness than it is to get permission'. Alternatively, select a room with hardly any chairs in the first place. Unused offices are good for this and have the added benefit that they are usually relatively small, which furthers the creation of a hot-house of ideas.

Another alternative is to do the session at the team board in much the same way that you would do a daily stand-up. This provides the benefit that the team board and all the team artefacts are right there in front of the team to use. Be aware of safety levels though: if the customer or manager or even other teams are close by, this proximity and potential lack of safety could inhibit people from offering sensitive yet important feelings and ideas.

This approach works very well when you have agreement from the group to explore a narrow subject area. It is great for root cause analysis (Five Whys for example) and for finding countermeasures. It is also very good where the retrospective session requires all the members to be actively theming and contributing to a solution, 'diverge and merge', for example.

Watch out for signs of fatigue. When people start to flag, get irritable or move away to find somewhere to sit down, that's a good cue that they've spent all their energy and need a break.

ALLOW SILENCE

An issue for many facilitators leading retrospectives is that they talk too much, because they are uncomfortable with silence. Facilitators often believe that their role in a retrospective is to help surface problems and encourage dialogue amongst the team. Inexperienced facilitators think that the best way to achieve this is to lead the discussion. The opposite is often true, and this applies both at the beginning of the session and at any time during the session.

In fact when the facilitator is the first to speak, team members can often be constrained from offering insights that they would otherwise have offered if given the time to find a suitable way of expressing them. We have experienced retrospectives where the facilitator's discomfort with silence has meant they filled any gap with an observation or a prompt to team members to talk. Such interjections are made with the best of intentions. However, the facilitator is not always in the best position to prompt people to express difficult insights. If the facilitator always leads the discussion, the team members might not develop the ability to raise difficult matters themselves.

When silence descends, it can appear to an observer that the people in the room are not interested in the retrospective and are just sitting there lifeless. In fact, the team members are really waiting for the right spark to start a tough conversation.

So if you find yourself facilitating a retrospective session where silence has fallen across the room, suppress the desire to speak and remove the awkwardness. Accepting the silence doesn't mean that the discomfort goes away. Instead the uneasiness shifts to the team members. It is exactly this feeling that will get the team to surface problems and engage in meaningful dialogue.

Key benefits

When the facilitator is quiet, conversation and insight are driven by the team rather than intentionally or unintentionally being steered by the facilitator.

This is a benefit because it means that the retrospective more accurately reflects the team's problems rather than those that the facilitator might choose to steer the retrospective towards. Having experienced (and facilitated) a fair few retrospective sessions, we can tell you, the facilitator does not always know best.

Even if the facilitator does have a good understanding of the topics that the team may choose to retrospect on, they should not relieve the team of their responsibility to truly look inward and reveal their thoughts. If the team surfaces the insights they will reach a greater depth of retrospection. The team members will develop the sense that they can unblock their own impediments and facilitate themselves.

Starting a retrospective with silence is in contrast to how many retrospectives start, with an icebreaker to get everyone talking. However, getting everyone talking and loosened up a bit may be papering over cracks that will get wider if not addressed.

Done successfully, allowing silence helps the team decrease their reliance on having a facilitator. It will ultimately move them closer to the goal of on-demand retrospection and continuous improvement.

How to make it work

Next time you are playing the role of facilitator in a retrospective session and you are uncomfortable with a silence in the room, check yourself and wait. As a facilitator, this requires you to have a certain level of consciousness about how much you speak during a session. Often reminding yourself of this as you enter a session is enough but also look for other triggers that can help you. Just silently asking yourself, 'when was the last time that you allowed silence in the session?' might help to raise your consciousness in this area.

Let the team members break the silence. Don't think of the period of silence as a game of chicken. Instead remind yourself that this is their session and their use of time. It is not your responsibility to provide content or even guarantee an outcome. Your goal is to foster teams that self-organise to solve their own problems and facilitate their own discussions.

Be aware of situations where the team and facilitator might not work closely together, especially if it is their first session together. In these instances the facilitator will probably have no insight into the team's situation. In addition, they might be stressed about standing in front of a new team. This combination of factors will amplify the discomfort that the facilitator feels during periods of silence compared to people who work together on a regular basis.

LET THE TEAM DICTATE DIRECTION

For many people facilitating a retrospective can be a daunting task, so we try to reduce the stress by planning thoroughly well in advance. But this can also be the downfall of facilitators who forget these very salient words of Winston Churchill: 'Plans are of little importance but planning is essential'.

In a retrospective session, we are asking a team of people to think about how they might improve. This is essentially an unpredictable process. We cannot and should not try to shackle this process with an over-prescriptive plan. Any attempt to do this will fail to deliver good results. Some retrospective session formats are indeed more likely to drive out specific types of improvement ideas over others. However, if we can't adapt the session to the team's view of their situation and their mood at that specific time, the team members will be constrained in putting forward their improvement ideas.

In addition, ignoring important points and discussion in favour of finishing the retrospective exactly to plan will result in disgruntled attendees. In our experience, scrum masters are most likely to fall foul of this pitfall. They tend to invest more time than others in preparation, and as process owners tend to follow protocol. We have experienced retrospectives where facilitators have viewed success as executing the plan to a T and on time yet there was no tangible output and where team members thought they were close to sorting out an issue but had to move on.

If you want to address the most pressing issues, don't just follow the pre-prepared plan. Instead allow the format to change to suit the feeling in the room and the direction that the conversation and ideas flow in. Remember that the point of any retrospective isn't to follow all the steps and activities of a plan, it is to drive out improvements however they come.

Key benefits

A facilitator who is skilled at going with the flow can draw out the biggest problems that the team currently faces as opposed to their own view of what was important when they made their plan.

People like to be heard, and when a facilitator acknowledges a divergent topic and encourages its exploration they gain more respect and potential influence. This could be important later when the facilitator might need their influence to finish on time with an actionable improvement idea.

How to make it work

We are not suggesting doing no preparation at all. Even very experienced facilitators prepare and plan a structure for how the session might flow, if not written down then at least in their heads. So continue to make plans for your retrospectives, just be prepared to adapt them at a moment's notice.

Look for signs that a retrospective session is not fitting with the team. Get used to spotting certain types of behaviour that should trigger a diversion from your plan. These might range from obvious cues like open disagreement with a particular discussion, the relevance of the format or activities, to behaviour such as gazing out of the window or looking at phones.

Such behaviours are warnings of disengagement, and rather than sticking to the plan hoping things improve and people re-engage, you should acknowledge the mood and change your approach.

If you didn't share the agenda to start with then you have the option to divert from the plan silently, using the building blocks you have practised to take the team on a different route. However if you have made the agenda explicit, it might be useful to acknowledge that it is not working for all in the room and ask the team if they would like to try something else.

Having options is the key to making this work. If the team members want to follow a path that isn't in your plan then having some 'go to' techniques to apply is very important. Have a notebook of retrospective ideas that you have used in the past and index it so you can access its contents quickly. Don't be afraid to flick through this during the session to jog your memory.

Learn key building blocks and fit them together on the fly as needed. For example dot voting and decider protocol are both decision-making tools; the simple thumbs-up-or-down of the latter is faster but doesn't provide for voting on several options very well. When the team need to make a decision, having these tools to hand to use at a moment's notice will produce a much smoother and ultimately more productive experience.

If you are reluctant to divert from the plan, when subjects come up that don't follow the direction you had planned, explicitly make a note of them and circulate them to the team after the session so that they can consider them outside the planned session. You might also want to have your own retrospective on your retrospective, to think about how you could have done things differently read the section *Check out as well as in*. This will help you to continually improve the way you facilitate retrospectives.

BE FREE INSIDE FENCES

Constraints are all around us. Acknowledging them can be the first step to solving the problems that they present. Often teams avoid stating constraints, as if the very act of discussing them will cause some exaggerated manifestation of them.

It is common for people to see constraints as inhibiting their creative ability, stopping them reaching their goals. It would seem logical to assume that the most creative ideas and designs come when people have no constraints at all placed on them. However there are many examples of how constraints have actually inspired people's best work. The architect Frank Gehry, best known for the Guggenheim Museum in Bilbao, Spain, and the Walt Disney Concert Hall in Los Angeles, where he worked to strict acoustic standards, is quoted as saying 'I think we turn those constraints into actions'. Having constraints removes options and with them the paralysis that too many options sometimes invokes.

In *Great Work*, David Sturt explains that constraints give us a starting point and some building blocks to work with. They are in fact foundational to creativity and innovation. They give us a puzzle to solve. A simple way to experience this is to run the *Marshmallow challenge*. Teams must build the tallest tower possible with the constraints that they have only spaghetti, one yard (roughly one meter) of tape, one yard of string and one marshmallow, which must be at the tower's summit. We have seen both passionate engagement and serious innovation when teams tackle this challenge.

Although constraints are very real in most workplaces, teams often don't explicitly acknowledge them or use them to push the envelope. They actually go to some lengths to avoid talking about constraints, even though all members of the team are aware that they are there. The constraints become the elephant in the room.

Don't fear constraints or try to ignore them. Instead make them visible, discuss them and use them as a stimulus to drive the team's innovation and improvement effort.

Key benefits

Explicitly discussing the main constraints a team faces generates a shared understanding of them. Team members are more likely to propose cohesive improvement ideas if they start from the same understanding of the constraints. Although diversity is good during the idea generation stage, convergence on an action to execute is important to ensure everyone is pulling in the same direction.

Stating the constraints faced and taking the time to get them all out in the open is cathartic and makes the challenge ahead feel much more achievable.

Once the constraints are explicitly stated, problem solvers naturally start to think of solutions. Stating the constraints leads to two further types of behaviour that we have regularly seen. Firstly, it encourages team members to question the validity of some constraints. This should lead to an effort to remove them rather than to work around them. Tom once worked with a team that questioned the stated constraint 'we have to use existing technologies'. Upon further discussion and a quick check with the lead architect, they established that there were actually hundreds of approved tools to choose from – not really a major constraint at all. Secondly, the problem solvers start coming up with hundreds of ways to reach their goals within the constraints that can't be quickly removed or are necessary. It is this collaboration and challenging of the boundaries that leads to major improvements and innovative breakthroughs.

How to make it work

Constraints are valid for a particular goal. Make sure that you specify a goal. This goal might be a specific software deliverable or it might be something more general like 'ship more features per month'.

Once the goal is explicit, go about brainstorming the constraints that the team members feel they face. Ask team members to spend about five minutes or until they run out of ideas, writing onto sticky notes (one per sticky) all the things that they believe to be their constraints. Ask team members not to vet what they write at this stage.

Go through them and remove duplicates. As you do so, mark those constraints that the team thinks should be challenged for removal rather than set as boundaries to work within. You can then usefully present these to senior people in your organisation who can remove the constraints – an excellent output from your session.

Ask the team to discuss how they are going to achieve their goal. Emphasise at this point that there are no stupid ideas. Some of the best improvement suggestions come from seemingly crazy beginnings, that are extended and evolved. Conduct this as an open discussion forum as this enables the ideas to start evolving immediately.

If you are facilitating the session, encourage the more unusual solutions and support team members in finding a way to make them work. Often the more experienced people within the team are limited by what they think is possible, constrained by their past experiences. Help the team to avoid shutting down ideas too soon. Ask the team 'what would it take to make this work?' and then start by solving the smaller issues.

LEARN FAST, DON'T FAIL FAST

Practices such as lean start-up promote the value of 'failing fast'. This catchy tag line is potentially harmful, because it's not the whole story. It isn't the failing that is important – we want to be successful. The important point is to learn fast.

Each improvement action a team runs is an opportunity to learn about how to overcome a problem and get better. An improvement idea is a hypothesis about something that might make us better. The improvement actions a team commit to executing are essentially experiments designed to prove or disprove the hypothesis. Once the actions have been completed, it is crucial that we learn the lessons.

Define success as something learnt, not only whether things actually improved. Don't repeat the same mistakes continually. Instead create an environment in which people take risks and recognise failures as opportunities to learn, not as something to be frowned on and stopped. To learn the lessons, retrospect on your retrospective actions.

Key benefits

Explicitly capturing the learning from improvement ideas closes the feedback loop surrounding the hypothesis. Teams reap the benefit of the learning gained so that they don't fail in the same way again. Performed in a thorough way, it enables the team to understand what part of a hypothesis was incorrect and can even lead them to retrospect on the process of forming future hypotheses.

When team members approach activities as learning opportunities, their mentality changes. Focusing on learning promotes the idea that an improvement idea might not be a success. It also teaches people to scrutinise the reasons and objectives behind the work they do. (It even encourages them not to assume that every requirement needs to be implemented.)

How to make it work

Spend time to dispel the misconception that we should be aiming to fail fast and that's all. Don't simply aim to fail fast. Aim to explicitly collect the information gained from failing – otherwise you will waste time and effort. Ensure that each improvement idea has an explicit assumption to validate or piece of uncertainty that it is aiming to reduce. This uncertainty could be a combination of two factors: whether the idea will actually make the world better and the cost of achieving that improvement.

Reduce uncertainty by running short and cheap experiments. If you have a problem with missing acceptance criteria, you might decide to try using specification by example for the next three months. Rather than committing the whole team to the experiment, start small with just part of the team for one story and wait for the results. As you start the experiment, define how you will be able to tell if it is a success. In the experiment to use specification by example you might choose to measure the amount of rework for a story completed in this way. After the experiment you can then compare this to the amount of rework you got with previous system, and you will have learnt something. If the hypothesis proved to be correct you might choose to roll it out further. Alternatively it could have failed and you could roll back to your original

way of working. As Bill Gates put it 'It's fine to celebrate success but it is more important to heed the lessons of failure'. If we don't take the time to understand and learn where we were wrong with an hypothesis, we will continue to make similar bad hypotheses.

Understand your learning by starting your next retrospective with a review. Review each improvement experiment and ask 'have the last retrospective actions been completed?', 'were they successful?' and 'what did we learn from completing those retrospective actions?'.

There is value in just stating the lessons learnt aloud in the group. This helps to build a shared understanding in the team which in turn will help the members make better choices in the future. If the team feels that discussing the learning is not enough, make the process more formal. Document the outcomes of all experiments either through new standard procedures or through explicit information. Make this information available to all teams and make it easily searchable. Putting it in a wiki is a good idea.

Ben worked with a group of teams who were developing a mobile social media application. The teams spent the first ten minutes of their retrospectives reflecting on their past actions and capturing the learning. To make individual teams' learning available to all the other teams, they held a 'retrospective of retrospectives'. In this session each team would share with the others what they had learnt from their previous improvement experiments. This led to a very nice chain of improvements where one team would had an improvement experiment that built on another's previous learning.

DON'T BE SCARED OF FREESTYLING IT

Scrum's clear definition and rules-driven nature is a good starting point for many teams. Similarly, taking a rules-based approach for retrospectives might be a good starting point, but as the context that the team works within changes, rules and processes might not fit so well. If a facilitator thinks they must always go into a retrospective with a plan, set of exercises or rule book to follow, they could be inhibiting the kind of spontaneous discussion that leads to innovation or discoveries.

Nothing should make you feel that a session doesn't count as a retrospective if it doesn't follow a plan in a book. Unfortunately we have met some facilitators who believe that unless the retrospective session follows an established format or technique, it cannot be deemed a retrospective. This is an unnecessary restriction on content and style. It's not about the format, it's about drawing out meaningful discussion about continuous improvement and generating ideas.

Not having variability in retrospective sessions constrains the generation of ideas. As we mentioned in the section *Keep switching your process*, just changing certain elements in a process, or worse still just changing the names of those elements (for example changing the three-point 'glad, mad, sad' wheel to a five-point 'start, stop, more of, less of, continue' wheel), will eventually lead to boring retrospectives where team members are disengaged.

Instead of following an established plan at your next retrospective, try freestyling it. Get together and just brainstorm or even chat through your problems without a structure, formal voting system or otherwise. Having no plan will not constrain the outcomes of your retrospectives. Welcome the informality that not having a plan brings.

Key benefits

Running a free-style retrospective every once in a while allows the team to reflect on their own maturity. It allows them to see that they own the retrospective. At this point the team transcend a rules-based approach, instead adopting a culture of continuous improvement. This in itself can be incredibly rewarding and motivating for the team and will permeate through to later regular retrospectives or, even better, to on-demand retrospectives.

If there's no plan at all, the facilitator can't subconsciously steer the session to suit the plan they had previously selected. This could mean that some potentially beneficial topics are discussed that might not have been if the plan had been followed. Even if you build a retrospective as you go along using tools from your toolbox, each module you employ has a mini-plan built in to it which could constrain the outcomes. Imagine that the team have written many sticky notes and the way that you've used this tool in the past says that you should now affinity-cluster them. What if the team don't see the need to do that as they instinctively know what they want to address? If you're not prepared to abandon the next step you could seriously hamper the team's flow. Freestyling avoids this, and saves time by not stepping through the process.

Not having a plan avoids patronising people by suggesting that the only way they could reach a useful outcome would be to follow a plan that someone else wrote. A lot of teams we've worked with have had their fill of buzzwords and fads, and they actively reject rebranded techniques based on principles that they have long held dear.

Freestyling a retrospective allows complete flexibility and responsiveness to the team's context at that point in time. No process could ever achieve this.

How to make it work

Not all situations require plans made ahead of time. Instead go to your session, introduce it as an opportunity to improve and let the team talk.

Mature teams in a safe environment will talk openly about how they can get better. As a facilitator your role isn't to follow the instructions of a set process. Your role is now to steer the team away from getting caught up in the effects of a problem and towards a tangible outcome or action to resolve it.

Keep a visual narrative of what is discussed. We find it is useful to capture discussion topics explicitly on sticky notes, put on the wall so team members can see them as the session unfolds. Having them visible allows the team to recap and to disagree if you have captured the meaning incorrectly. If you attempt to do this in a private notepad, team members may think you are recording other observations, which will lead to a loss of safety in the room.

Be aware that often it can be useful to have plans. A plan is particularly helpful when team and facilitator are unfamiliar with one another or maybe where the team members or facilitator are not used to retrospecting at all. In these instances having a toolbox of techniques and tools at hand will certainly help when people are lost.

Finally, keep an eye on the clock. As the session draws to an end, make sure you encourage the team to focus on identifying some actionable outcome. You should have some good discussion reflected on the wall, often already in the form of ideas for actions or experiments. A word of warning though, although these may appear to be well formed, choosing one can often take longer than you expect.

FACILITATING SESSIONS

CREATE A RETROSPECTIVE MENU

Retrospective discussions can often wander from the plan as the team explores interesting topics. Imagination and free thinking should be given some space, but the session still needs to move along. If the lateral discussion is one-sided or the retrospective does not conclude with improvement actions, the session will be disappointing to attendees. To allow exploration away from a fixed agenda while still ensuring a good outcome, create a list of building blocks for the fundamental parts of your retrospectives, the general activities that drive a session towards a successful conclusion. Fill in the blocks with techniques that can help you facilitate sessions, and keep the list handy so you can easily propose an appropriate technique when the discussion starts moving in an unplanned direction.

For example, here are the building blocks on our list:

- *Making group decisions*: Teams need to choose between options, decide whether to continue discussing a certain topic or agree on a course of action.
- *Venting*: People need the opportunity to let off steam from time to time and get things off their chest.
- *Level setting*: Team members need to set expectation levels, baseline principles and agreements.
- *Prioritising*: Groups need to pick topics to discuss and select ideas to implement.
- *Stopping side-tracked discussion*: Having a way to move conversation along can save time and frustration.
- *Root cause analysis*: Teams may need guidance to discover the real causes of their problems.
- *Ensuring safety, openness and inclusion*: Openness and discussion safety lead to a diverse range of ideas, foster collaboration and motivate people.

Key benefits

A reference list of building blocks helps facilitators adapt easily to the unfolding events. When the team members want to take the session away from the initial agenda, the facilitator still has a pool of resources to offer suggestions for reaching a good retrospective outcome. A varied toolbox enables facilitators to combine different exercises, keeping the team members interested and engaged.

A list of building blocks allows the team members to learn about facilitation techniques, so they can improve their own discussions and remove some of the need for an external facilitator.

How to make it work

Analyse past retrospectives, focusing on the purpose behind each activity. Avoid listing individual exercises that make up the format, such as Sailboat or Starfish, but instead capture the outcomes and the intent behind using those exercises. The common patterns that emerge are good candidates for the building blocks. After identifying the basic blocks, list the options for the techniques that fit each block.

Make this list easily accessible – for example on a public wiki page. Improve the list after each new retrospective, add information about the situations where a technique worked well or did not work well.

Write a crib sheet that summarises your building blocks and techniques. Keep the sheet with you when facilitating retrospectives, so you can use it to guide the team and select techniques.

As a kick-start, here are some example techniques for the building blocks on our list:

Make group decisions using the decider protocol from *Software for Your Head*. Team members vote with their thumbs to conclude a proposal. Thumbs up for a firm yes, down for no and flat if neutral or unsure. Ask what it would take for the naysayers to become supporters.

For venting, we like the two-minute time-box: give each participant two minutes for a monologue. Another option is Donning the Red Hat from De Bono's *Six Thinking Hats*.

When level setting, try checking in against your rules: ask the team members to show, with a simple thumbs up or thumb down, if they will abide by the current team meeting rules. If not, review the meeting principles quickly, for example using the ideas explained in the section *Renew your vows*.

For prioritising, try dot-voting: get the participants to mark dots against their preferred options on a whiteboard or a flip-chart. Another prioritisation technique is x-y axes: get the group to discuss actions and rank them along two axes. For example, prioritise improvement suggestions by cost on one axis and by expected impact on another.

Stop side-tracked conversations with move on cards: give a playing card to each participant to show during a conversation if they feel the discussion is going nowhere. Once a single person shows their card, ask the others if they would like to play theirs. If the majority then show their cards, it's time to move on. This can work well when used with a parking lot of topics to suspend for now, but revisit later. Similarly, use an egg timer to enforce a time-box, after which the majority decides whether to continue discussing the current topic or move on.

Tackle root cause analysis using five whys, which we described in the section *Don't just say we can't*. An alternative technique is the *Ishikawa (Fishbone)*. We also like the adapted fishbone method for software using six Ms: method, (hu)man (brain) power, management, measurement, materials and machine.

To ensure safety, openness and inclusion, remind people about Norm Kerth's prime directive at the start of a session. Another option is to check the room temperature: gauge people's feelings towards having an open discussion. Ask the participants to anonymously note down a score from 1 to 5 (1 being 'I don't want to talk about anything right now', 3 being 'I'll discuss some things but not others' and 5 being 'I'll talk openly about anything'). If there are any scores less or equal to 3, discussing safety concerns can be more productive in the long run than just ploughing ahead.

DON'T LET IMPEDIMENTS BECOME PERMANENT

Some impediments are a temporary hindrance or obstruction to the flow of work, whereas others can become a permanent part of the environment and are much harder to change. The longer an impediment remains unchallenged, the greater the chance that a team will begin accepting it as part of the furniture, start working round it and stop trying to fix it. When an impediment becomes an accepted permanent fixture of the environment, the team has wittingly or unwittingly chosen to become less effective in the long-term. The more these long-term impediments build up, the less productive a team becomes. Over time, if more impediments emerge than the team can remove, team morale plummets.

Don't let impediments become permanent. Be alert to them, identify impediments during retrospectives and look for those that repeat or reappear. Pay specific attention to issues that emerge repeatedly, find out how long they have existed and spend time assessing the impact of allowing them to remain unchecked. Keep impediments visible, compare them side by side and look for themes and patterns.

Key benefits

Teams who are explicitly aware of their impediments can spot new problems early, before such issues become harder constraints. When a team compares impediments side by side, they can more quickly select those that will be easier and more beneficial to resolve.

By visualising impediments and making stakeholders aware of such issues, teams have a better chance to involve decision makers and get support for resolving organisational and environmental problems. Management might start to see patterns, such as specific areas of the business where they need to lend support and exert some influence. The sheer volume of impediments can also be a stark awakening and catalyst for action, particularly when it is the surrounding organisation that is blocking a team, and they have been unable to influence it.

Measuring or valuing impediments enables clear and focused discussion with stakeholders about the costs and benefits for removing them. This can help create some slack to tackle the problems, even versus delivering business features, because removing impediments should enable better delivery in future.

How to make it work

Capture impediments as they emerge, in daily stand-up meetings, in planning, in retrospectives and throughout the working day. Keep a visible log of impediments in the team area and keep them up to date, scratching out those that have been addressed and remembering to check for offenders that reoccur. Run an instant retrospective about any repeating impediments. One team we worked with devised a rule of three, whereby the third time something happened, they would always retrospect on it there and then.

The distinction between a temporary impediment and a permanent one is not always crystal clear. The way we distinguish between them is based on several criteria, such as:

- the length of time it has been present
- whether a team can resolve it on their own
- the amount of effort and complexity involved in resolving it
- the number of failed attempts to remove it

Another approach we find valuable is to run a retrospective that focuses on highlighting all the major impediments that affect the team. Assess whether each impediment is temporary or permanent and then prioritise them. To do this, express each one against a set of criteria, for example their impact on throughput, lead time, quality or morale. Then weigh each one up for its cost and ease of removal, using the bullet point list above as a stimulus. You could use absolute values if known, alternatively a score between 1 and 10, or size them relative to each other using the Fibonacci scale. Multiply the values to arrive at a priority score, which is a token for a discussion about which ones to tackle first. As part of that discussion, note down what it would take to remove each impediment along with how empowered the team feels to remove it themselves or if anyone is needed to help unblock it.

Encourage stakeholders to talk with the team about these impediments. Have a conversation about the impact and priority of these issues, discuss potential experiments to test how they might be resolved and any support that management can provide. Even if you've used a relative scale to prioritise impediments, collect data to quantify them. This will facilitate more fruitful discussion about why they should be removed and what activities and support are required, effectively building a business case.

Visualise the details of the impediment you are addressing, as well as the experiments being run. The hypotheses, assumptions and the expected results can form a PDCA board (Plan, Do, Check, Act), which can be used to engage in regular continuous improvement cycles with management. As Michael and Freddy Balle describe in *Lead with Respect*, visualising experiments and recording outcomes and observations with a PDCA board can stimulate management into going to *gemba* (Japanese for the place where value is created – that is, the shop floor, or in our case, the team's work area).

When management are engaged in the specifics of daily work, they can challenge the team about why they are running the experiments they are, what impediments they hope to remove and understand more about the challenges. Keep this as a regular interaction about real problems. Management will gain a much greater understanding of engineering standards and real challenges to them. Those impediments marked as permanent are the real gauntlet laid down for management. If the team doesn't think they can remove such impediments, management can challenge the team's ability to influence the organisation or try to tackle the problems themselves.

RE-ENERGISING
RETROSPECTIVES

DO A FACE-TO-FACE TEAM 360

Giving personal feedback is often overlooked during retrospectives. Teams tend to focus on process or technical issues while ignoring human ones. This means that opportunities for personal improvement are lost or left to an annual appraisal process where feedback could come second-hand through a line manager.

Giving and receiving personal feedback can be a very difficult thing. For feedback to be effective, the recipient has to trust that it is given with good intention, as a constructive observation. The giver of feedback also has to trust that the receiver will receive it in that manner. This level of trust can be hard to achieve and for some just does not come naturally at all.

Trust cannot be demanded or forced, it is built over time. Often a good level of trust may not be reached because team members do not have an environment where they feel safe enough to expose their vulnerabilities. It is much easier to talk safely about processes and technical improvements because these are not personal in nature, nor likely to drive strong emotional responses and cause conflict.

A useful technique to encourage personal improvement is team 360 feedback. Encourage everyone to give feedback on everyone else, each person in turn becomes the subject of feedback: going round the room, each of the other team members gives feedback while the receiving person notes down whatever they wish to take away and work on. Make sure to time-box the session so that everyone gets enough time and no-one gets rushed at the end or misses her turn for feedback.

The main aim of this technique is to provide richer and more rounded feedback by the inclusion of many different perspectives. The key to this particular type of 360 feedback is the face-to-face aspect. Make it

expected and desirable to give feedback directly and in front of the rest of the team, as part of the retrospective.

Key benefits

Because the expected norm is to provide feedback, opting out of doing it becomes very hard. The point isn't to make people feel socially awkward, it is to overcome the initial discomfort, enabling personal feedback to become acceptable and forge better understanding. Ultimately it allows people to give feedback they would not have been comfortable initiating otherwise.

A significant benefit of this one is that, over a few runs, it becomes much less awkward to say what needs to be said. Sometimes the pursuit of continuous improvement brings with it the need to surface some sensitive issues.

This idea helps make those conversations possible and hopefully lets criticism be given and taken in a constructive manner. If the each team member expects to give and receive direct and specific feedback, avoiding it becomes an effort.

The strength that the team gains from this form of feedback is immense. It may feel strange and uncomfortable to start with, but when it is understood that the purpose of all the feedback is to make the team better, these feelings quickly fall away. Do not forget the positive feedback that team members receive. This appreciation strengthens the team bond and ultimately helps each member understand where on the field they play best for the team.

When the 360 feedback happens regularly, it reduces the potential for a pressure-cooker explosion, where unsaid feedback can leave feelings simmering away for weeks and months, which can be very damaging to a team. The face-to-face nature of this feedback breeds trust. As a member of a team receiving this type of feedback, I know where I am, all my team members have been honest with me and it is now up to me what I do with that feedback.

How to make it work

A technique that we've found works very well is for team members to give one strength, one example where they felt the individual did well, and one specific area for improvement. Other variations of this can be for each participant to score themselves against criteria and the team to mediate their scoring with its consensus being revealed at the end. You will hear things like, 'John, I don't think that you are a 4 in that, Sally has herself as a 4 in that and I don't think you are quite at Sally's level'. In this technique, the criteria make the feedback more objective. A possible drawback is that a criterion is too specific and team members could be restricted on the scope of the feedback that they give. In addition, if in using this technique, it turns into a tick-box exercise with no discussion of the reasoning, most of the value is lost.

For a bonus point, try including the coach, facilitator or Scrum master, provide them with feedback and receive a different perspective on the team.

Here are some other tips for giving and receiving face-to-face 360 feedback:

- The only acceptable answer to feedback is 'thank you'. Don't defend your position, this may prevent further feedback.
- Saying 'thank you' is very powerful. Appreciation will grow trust and strengthen the team bond.
- Use concrete examples. This makes feedback more impactful, more genuine and easier to understand and cement in the mind.
- After the retrospective, refer to someone independent for their opinion on controversial feedback.
- The subject of the feedback might open with an honest assessment of themselves. People tend to be harder on themselves than others, but being self-critical makes feedback from the rest of the team more easy to handle.
- Provide feedback in a sandwich format: two slices of appreciation around an improvement filling.
- As team members get more trusting with each other, use Atkins feedback (no bread, just the meat in the middle).
- Similarly, make the positive feedback related to the improvement idea 'I like this.... you could improve it by.....'.

TAILOR YOUR RETROSPECTIVES

When you are planning a retrospective it's really helpful to bear in mind what's going on that is affecting the team. By considering the current context and mood of the team it is possible to avoid picking a retrospective session that goes down like a lead balloon.

We once attended a retrospective where a team had made a delivery just two days earlier. There had been a defect in the software released and they had spent the last 48 hours trying to limit the damage. The people in question were always very diligent and had taken the defect very seriously. Everyone in the team hurried along to the retro, keen to address the issue. When they arrived the scrum master cheerfully stated that the team would be doing an 'appreciation retrospective' that he had seen online, where the participants all thank each other for being great. Not surprisingly, everyone was amazed and disappointed.

If you fail to take account of the context and focus retrospectives on what has just happened you risk the team members disengaging. They might also miss out on vital learning and even the chance to counteract what has happened.

The solution is to make sure you keep retrospectives relevant to recent events, while also targeting them towards specific purposes.

Key benefits

If you tailor your retrospectives to the current team and events they will engage team members much more. In our experience, people appreciate a retrospective that targets a specific event. If it was significant then they will be sure to want to talk about and learn from it.

The results will almost certainly be better, as you will be covering the things that are affecting the team most.

Tailoring your retrospectives to current events keeps them interesting. In our experience teams really do appreciate variety in retrospectives. In addition the extra effort spent by the facilitator influences them to make more effort themselves.

How to make it work

Build up a personal armoury of different types of retrospective. Keep notes on where you have used them, an outline of what you did and tips for running them. Also note how well they were received. Once you have a catalogue of retrospective experiences, keep your eye on what is going on in the team and choose a format to suit the team's current situation. For the team mentioned previously it might have been better to use a root cause analysis retrospective to inspect the defect introduced during their recent release. Consider different aspects of the team's health: quality of delivery, speed, predictability, team dynamics, discipline. This doesn't mean picking the aspect that you want to influence most for your own agenda and planning the retro around that.

Where you think an event merits inspection propose it and see if the team agree it is worth pursuing.

There are various types of retrospective to choose from, though many are of the same type, just with slightly different formats. For example, formats such as mad, sad, glad, starfish, sailboat are variations that allow us to categorise positives, negatives and learning. Here are our seven categories of retrospective:

- *No fixed context:* mad, sad, glad or sailboat. Using different prompts to drive out positives, negatives and learning; actions driven by team voting on what matters most at that time.
- *Root cause analysis:* Dissect a story, five whys. Focusing on specific issues that have arisen, maybe in a story delivered or a production defect. Typically quite a narrow scope with a view to resolving and guarding against similar occurrences.

- *Team dynamics:* Do a face-to-face team 360, appreciation retro. Focusing on relationships, collaboration and inter-personal improvement.
- *Team maturity:* Compare against models, not teams, XP radar. Assessing the team's progress, discipline, maturity and standards of practice using a framework.
- *Ways of working:* Renew your vows, team behaviour model. Agreeing the overall rules and values the team abides by; discussing, setting or revisiting the ways of working, team principles and values in order to set expectations, allow better self-regulation and improve understanding amongst the team members.
- *Changing the lens:* Review projects with a larger group, Walk the value stream. Using broader dimensions, such as the length of time of a project; thinking from the perspective of the work to change the way we view our working environment and step back from everyday team activities.
- *Protecting the future:* 'futurespective', failure mode and effect analysis. Looking forward and predicting potential problems so that you can guard against them in the here and now.

Having a list of the options can help you to select the most appropriate format for a particular session. In our experience, when team members know what the options are they start to request specific types of retrospective as they learn which ones work best for them in specific circumstances.

Lastly, as ever context is king, and as clichéd as it sounds, people are different, so no single format will consistently please all of the people all of the time, so be prepared to get different reactions even when applying a format to similar events. Inspect and adapt!

CELEBRATE GOOD TIMES

Our human nature means we genuinely want to please others around us with the products we build, the tasks we perform. But there is nothing worse than working hard without any recognition. In fact, this actually leads to decreased motivation and reduced performance.

All too often teams miss the opportunity to celebrate a job well done. If there is a constant pressure to deliver to tight deadlines the chance to celebrate can be missed. A lack of appreciation will have damaging effects if it is allowed to continue over the longer term.

Take opportunities to celebrate success within your team or department. Small successes don't need big shindigs. Small and frequent celebrations such as sharing cakes, doughnuts or healthier snacks are great for those smaller occasions and serve to remind us that we are making progress and performing good work.

For the bigger achievements, set aside some money and put thought into arranging something special that the whole team will love, even if just for the knowledge that someone really appreciates the job they are doing.

At this point we should ground this idea a little bit, as it can be very contextual. If your team has recently moved from six-monthly releases to monthly releases, celebrating a monthly release is perfectly reasonable. The counter argument however, could be that releasing software is just doing your job, so be sensitive to the relationships with other teams and stakeholders you work with.

If your team gets down to weekly, daily or even intra-day releases, you might also get very sick of cake and doughnuts if you keep celebrating. Teams reach an interesting situation when every day is a no-news day. Releases happen all the time, small improvements go on

all the time, but not large enough to warrant a fanfare. At this point you should look at celebrating making key impacts, reaping benefits or learning.

It is important that those who have the respect of the team take the opportunity to celebrate success. We have found that an off-site location adds more significance to the occasion and makes it much more vivid and memorable for the team members.

Giving rewards often, especially if they are expected, has the opposite effect to what people intend. In *Drive*, Dan Pink writes that such rewards kill intrinsic motivation. However in contrast, unexpected rewards, given as an act of appreciation by those whom the team respects, do not undermine an individual's intrinsic motivation.

Key benefits

Unexpected rewards and celebrations show the team that the giver appreciates what they have done and has thought specifically about how best to celebrate the team's successes. That appreciation and effort to please motivates the team members, and makes them happier, energised and eager to improve.

Celebrations serve to bring the whole team closer together and any opportunity to do that is worth its weight in gold.

Displaying appreciation as an embedded part of the team and organisational culture is great for improving staff retention.

Celebrations provide a super opportunity to tighten the communication loop, discuss ideas and challenges and to align everyone more closely to a shared vision.

How to make it work

Although celebrating success seems obvious and easy, it needs to be done in the right way. If it is done incorrectly, even good intentions may end up being viewed negatively.

The obvious ways to celebrate are things like buying cake, taking everyone out for a meal or drinks or organising an activity such as bowling. These are all good ideas. However the subtleties of a good celebration lie in its execution.

When you pick a celebration, be careful to pick something that is attractive to the whole team. For example, some people might not want to eat cake, some people might not choose to drink, so find something that all team members will be keen to engage in. Yes, it does require thought, and yes, it does mean we need to know our team well!

That said, and counterintuitively (to us at least), we wouldn't advocate asking the team members' opinions on what they would like to do. We have seen these potentially joyous occasions implode because of poor expectation management. If the team members are canvassed for ideas beforehand, different ideas might be in competition with one another and certain team members might feel disgruntled when their idea isn't chosen. Believe it or not, we have even seen teams that have wanted to split and have two different celebrations at separate venues.

For those teams who are continuously delivering, we have found that it works nicely to align celebration to the impact the software is having, rather than the delivery of software. Lots of small software releases build to have an increasing impact on the business and once a significant level of impact is achieved, that is the time to celebrate.

The key to good execution is that it demonstrates that the manager or leader, a person whom the team members respect, has really thought about how to please them. This has much more value than just giving cash or a voucher or some other cursory gift. In fact, as a manager or leader, making the time to go with the team really shows how much it means.

KEEP SWITCHING YOUR PROCESS

Rigidly following the same retrospective steps again and again will become uninspiring, for both team and facilitator. Eventually this can kill engagement and ultimately the quality of output from your sessions.

The five-step process 'set the stage, gather data, generate insights, decide what to do and close', described by Derby and Larsen in the book *Agile Retrospectives: Making Good Teams Great* has proven invaluable for so many teams we've known. However, its popularity has also led to it becoming the only way that many people plan and run retrospectives. This could stifle their success and longevity, as the process can start to feel mechanical. In teams we have worked with, on more than one occasion we have heard 'it doesn't matter what process you choose, it's all the same thing'.

No matter the format or process used, if retrospectives are not varied then expect the number and scope of improvement ideas generated to be limited too.

If the team know what is coming, they will have a good idea about what they will say and how they will vote during the obligatory dot-voting that will follow. This pre-meditation and predictability is not conducive to innovative thinking. Turning up with pre-canned answers to problems risks people not using the retrospective session itself to explore ideas. This will constrain opportunities to learn and innovate. If the team members are not stretched to expand their horizons and think more radically then arguably there is little point in retrospectives where everyone is just going through the motions.

Avoid stagnation by building a repertoire of process ideas and retrospective building blocks that you can rotate and customise to suit the needs and context of the team. These will become an essential resource to draw on. A varied toolkit can bring success by allowing adaption to specific circumstances.

Retrospectives should be engaging and provide a bit of a recharge at the end of an iteration or period of time. Keep switching the process you use to run retrospectives in order to energise the participants.

Key benefits

Changing the types of process steps and the order of them is a technique to keep your retrospective sessions fresh, energetic and generating sack-loads of good ideas. Using a wider range of retrospective process steps is more likely to generate more varied and higher quality improvement ideas. There is likely to be higher attendance and less of the 'can we postpone it because' excuses.

Building a repertoire involves researching new ideas and sources of inspiration. This will lead you to unconventional building blocks that on the face of it may not seem immediately applicable to a team's current needs. However, in the future these building blocks might eventually yield a rare gem that helps discover some ground-breaking improvement ideas.

When your personal repertoire dries up, and you have wrung everything you can from this book and reached the end of the Internet, start making up your own building blocks. This in itself is incredibly rewarding as it creates the opportunity to tailor retrospectives to events happening at the time and to the specific team aspirations and culture.

How to make it work

List the different steps in your retrospective process and try and vary these. Also try inviting different people or going to a different place. There are plenty of other examples in this book.

Some retrospective processes are worth repeating. For example, using a team maturity retrospective, like the one described in the section *Compare against models, not teams*, on an intermittent basis will enable you to see the change in the team's competencies over time.

Doing some prep for retrospective sessions can pay dividends. No-one should view these session as a tax on their time and that includes the facilitator. Take the time to research some fresh ideas, talk to others around you and use the Internet.

Build your own library. Fill it with process building blocks, as well as different formats and exercises. We like to keep our own notebook for retrospective ideas and building blocks, proven (through trial and error) over many years. In fact much of this book is drawn from it. We keep notes about the results from many of the retrospectives we have run, including what method we used, any preparation required, how long it took, how many people attended and any specific detail about the context and outcomes.

For example, Ben once delivered a retrospective to a group of 25 people around the world via telepresence. It was the end of a successful project and he used a format which involved gathering and collating data ahead of time. He also made notes on where he got positive outputs and those where he felt the technique was challenged. You can read more detail on this in the section *Review projects with a larger group*.

RE-ENERGISING RETROSPECTIVES

KEEP IT SHORT

Sometimes it can be hard to drive to a specific action or outcome during a retrospective. Although it can be valuable to do a retrospective that just level sets people's expectation, those that identify improvement ideas and actions are the ones that will make measurable improvements to the way you work.

It might be hard to reach a tangible outcome in some retrospectives, because agreement on action takes an excessively long time. This could be due to the fact that the people involved feel passionately about the subject in question and everyone wants to contribute their opinion. While this is valuable up to a point, teams should strive to make sessions as effective as possible.

Alternatively it could be that teams don't reach an outcome at all. They let the session drift, with the hope that there is a concrete action just round the corner. The result can be that they either run out of time, or worse, lose the will to try and improve.

When sessions regularly don't result in generating specific improvement actions, the team is missing the full potential of continuous improvement. In much the same way that a skilled meeting facilitator keeps all their meetings concise and focused, keep your retrospective sessions brief and focused on actions.

Key benefits

If we can manage to reach the same outcome from the retrospective session in less time we are economically better off. A shorter duration sets a focus on a drive towards actions. This will edge participants away from circular conversations and any reluctance to commit to solid actions.

A short and focused retrospective session gives teams a sense of urgency and purpose. They take these qualities away with them, back to their work. When we have cut the length of retrospective sessions, we have seen many teams leave the retrospective room within twenty minutes and spend the remaining timetabled time actually implementing their improvement idea. This significantly increases the proportion of ideas that get implemented by teams.

As the retrospective session is quicker and costs less, teams are much more willing to repeat the retrospective process more often. With the transaction cost of running the session greatly reduced, teams can design and test an experiment faster. They can then repeat this loop more times in a given period.

The result is a team that improves faster than they otherwise would with longer retrospectives. Not only does this allow the team to complete more improvement experiments, it also drives them nicely towards a more continuous retrospection and improvement process.

How to make it work

Start by halving the length of your retrospective. Retain the safety check or an ice-breaker at the beginning if the team need it. Make the objective of the session clear and concise, try something like 'We are here to retrospect and pick an actionable way to move the team forward to working in a better way'.

The team might be worried that they will not have time to consider their improvement options before they make a choice. At this point remind them that they have thousands of continuous improvement cycles ahead of them. As Jarod Kintz famously said 'When faced with two equally tough choices, most people choose the third choice: to not choose.' Don't let the team fall into the same trap. Point out that they do not have to pick the perfect idea, they just have to pick something.

As a facilitator, just make sure that the team members are driving towards an action and that they are aware of the time. We like to take a laptop with a countdown timer on the screen so that team members can check the remaining time themselves. It may still be useful to prompt them every five or ten minutes if they get drawn into deep conversation.

Ben cut the length of a teams retrospective session to great effect when he worked with a charity organisation. They were new to running retrospective sessions to reflect on their non-technical project work. The team spent a long time getting stuck in weighing up their options for actions. They were effectively doing analysis and running hundreds of 'what if' scenarios during the sessions without reaching a decision. The simple act of cutting the time and not allowing this level of discussion led to more improvement actions being attempted and a much less frustrated team.

Be careful not to go too far the other way. Rushing the team to an outcome could mean they end up with a superficial experiment that they do not believe to be worthy of their time. If participants are panicked, they will just pick something without any consideration. Alternatively they may even game the idea and pick something really quickly in order to get back to their other work. Also be conscious of the softer benefits that come from longer sessions. It can often be beneficial to let people rant and get things off their chest.

To avoid a rush, book your retrospective session for longer than you intend it to run for. This will allow you to overrun your intended slot and ease the pressure if participants seem too rushed. One way to check that the team members are not falling foul of this trap is to *Use numbers to help gauge success*.

SWITCH YOUR FACILITATORS AROUND

Even with the best of intentions, it is easy for a team and facilitator to become comfortable and to avoid rocking the boat for fear of capsizing the team. This means that they may miss the chance to tackle difficult problems that, if fixed, would really move them forward.

A possibly more alarming consideration is that regular pairings of teams and facilitator can gradually become desensitised to the presence of a particular problem, as in the boiling frog syndrome.

If a team has the same regular facilitator, they might even end up in a position where they feel that the facilitator could actually be part of a problem. In this circumstance the team members are unlikely to feel comfortable discussing the facilitator in their presence.

Although it may be beneficial for the facilitator to have some knowledge of the dynamics of the group they are working with, it can also be beneficial for the team to get a fresh viewpoint every once in a while. Take the opportunity to switch facilitators and teams around.

Key benefits

First and most simply, varying the facilitator brings more variety in how retrospectives are run. This will ultimately drive out fresh improvement ideas. Even if the format or routine stays the same the style that the new facilitator has is likely to be enough to mix it up.

Secondly, the fresh eyes that the new facilitator brings can give new insights. Often these new insights are in an area which the team members and regular facilitator have not considered before.

Having a new facilitator encourages the team to address any long-standing problem they have, an elephant in the room which even a mature facilitator and team pairing may have chosen to avoid. The new facilitator will have less understanding of why things are the way they are. This perspective is a good thing as it enables them to call things out with impunity.

If the team normally has a dedicated facilitator, bringing in someone different once in a while gives the members the chance to retrospect on their relationship with their usual facilitator in a neutral and safe setting. This independence allows the team to highlight possible areas where the relationship with their regular facilitator could be improved.

For the facilitator, an occasional switch is a great opportunity to challenge themselves by working with different teams and even different departments.

How to make it work

This is reasonably easy to achieve. It just requires a prompt for teams to take the chance and some organisation to arrange it to happen.

So that the change in facilitators does not come as a surprise, take time to set it as a regular occurrence. This helps make sure that no one feels they are being rejected, or that someone else is trying to muscle in on their turf.

If you have more than one facilitator, swapping them between teams should be very simple and just require some diary coordination.

For a retrospective at the end of a project or any with elements of a political nature, it can be beneficial to have an external facilitator. We have seen this work effectively by asking someone from another department of the organisation to help. It might even be worth getting someone from outside the organisation to run the retrospective. If you have an external facilitator, ask the team's regular facilitator to attend too if it seems likely that their perspective will prove useful.

We did this successfully when working at a large financial institution. We were asked to help the teams in a department reset their way of working. The first step we took was to hold a series of large retrospectives. Not having any knowledge of the teams meant that our questioning appeared very naive. However the actions that were driven out took a common theme 'investigate why...'. This happened because many questions that were raised by participants and facilitators alike, had no definitive answer.

When a team is in a session with a new facilitator and they choose to retrospect on their relationship with their regular facilitator, obviously the new facilitator needs to be wary. As caretaker facilitator you must encourage an environment where the team members feel safe to speak their mind in your presence. For example, they should not feel that you will take any information to your colleague. You must be very careful not to defend their usual facilitator's position, even though you might identify with it. As the facilitator of this session you should help the team frame the output in a way that is constructive for the relationship in the future. If everyone leaves the room with the shared belief that the relationship is not working, but there is no plan to rectify the situation, you have not achieved much. If you focus on actions that will improve the relationship, you are also likely to avoid anyone having the perception that other participants are bad-mouthing about them.

PLAY RETROSPECTIVE ROULETTE

Teams often have members who are incredibly vocal and press their points of view at each retrospective. These team members disproportionately influence the content and direction of the retrospective towards their views of what the team's biggest problems are. In the worst case we have seen individuals direct the topics for discussion to suit their own agenda, rather than in the interest of the team.

Less vocal team members who do not feel comfortable raising issues might not contribute valuable insights to the retrospective. Arguing for the issues they want to talk about over a more vocal and forceful person can be very hard and even distressing. It is much easier and safer to go with the flow and accept what those louder voices want to discuss.

If team members only discuss a limited range of topics, retrospectives become repetitive and lose value.

One fun way to ensure variability is to randomly select ideas, instead of letting team members vote on them. This technique is called retrospective roulette.

Key benefits

Using retrospective roulette means that every idea suggested has the same chance of being discussed. This means that discussion is more diverse and you won't lose valuable ideas. Teams tend to get particularly interesting discussion on points of view that are potentially niche or not widely shared. We worked with a team in a financial services client that used retrospective roulette to great effect. The team that chose to use this technique regularly had much

more diverse retrospectives than their counterparts that didn't use it. They produced many great outcomes by shedding new light on obstacles to improvement and obtaining better shared understanding of each other's opinions. It was particularly effective at drawing out observations from the junior members of the team.

Playing retrospective roulette is also a chance to let off some steam by turning the session into a game. This fun approach helps to keep the retrospectives fresh, which encourages greater attendance and participation.

You can save time on the prioritisation and selection of ideas to discuss. Randomly selecting topics during the session will be far quicker than dot voting or using another prioritisation technique.

How to make it work

Before the retrospective, have team members register their topics for discussion. This could be as simple as emailing ideas to the facilitator ahead of time or more publicly by writing them on a sheet in the team area. Experiment with having team members emailing them as they occur to them or batching them and emailing them all just before the session. Ben once worked with a team who even had an automated collection bot in their team messaging channel hosted on their collaboration tool. They set up the bot to collect anything following a particular identifying command. Team members could then quickly log topics they thought of during the sprint.

If people are inhibited about raising issues publicly then collating ideas anonymously is also possible. To do

this try having the facilitator anonymise ideas sent by email or use an online survey that allows a free text response. However, when these ideas are discussed the team members will have to interpret them as the contributor will not give an introduction.

If you have more than 36 suggestions, try removing duplicate suggestions. If after doing this you still have more than 36, select some at random to carry over to the next game. This might help you include more ideas in the game. As a facilitator, be careful when you remove duplicate suggestions. If you wrongly assume that two ideas are the same and remove one of them, the team member will be annoyed that their views are not being included. To avoid this, do the groundwork and ask for clarification at the start of the retrospective. If you do not remove duplicate entries, you end up with a roulette wheel weighted proportionally to the number of people who raised a particular subject, which gives a greater chance of covering a hot topic.

Once collected, log each idea and the name of the person or people who raised them against a number from 1 to 36.

Have the list of numbers, names and ideas up on the wall for all to see. This creates more excitement as team members cheer on their favourite discussion topic when the wheel is spun.

At this point you are probably asking yourself 'who has access to a roulette wheel?', but they are relatively cheap to buy. Alternatively there are plenty of applications available for tablets and smartphones.

When the ball settles on a number, ask whoever raised the idea to introduce it. Run a lean coffee approach by time-boxing the discussion to a short period of time (say seven minutes) and then ask the team members to vote to move on or continue with a simple thumbs up or down. If people want to move on and they haven't already settled on an improvement action, ask them for a concrete action before starting the next spin. Continue spinning until your budgeted time has run out.

If you get a blank ask the spinner to spin the wheel again or, to make the session more interesting, ask them to tell everyone a fact about themselves that the team don't already know (this rule needs to be known in advance). This may seem superficial but it actually has the nice effect that it brings the team closer together. Be careful not to let the session get derailed though.

Add to the excitement by having a special prize if you hit a zero (house win). We have worked with teams where they would decamp to the pub if the house won.

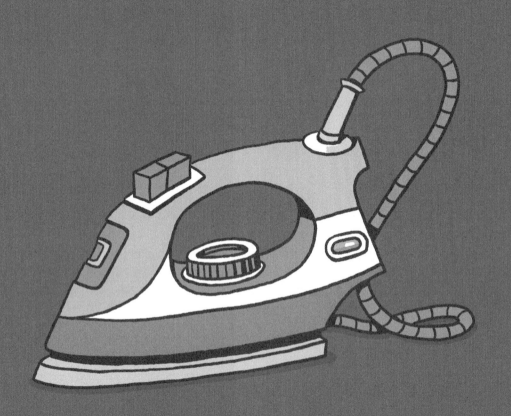

IMPROVING
OUTCOMES

CREATE A BUSINESS CASE

Teams can have some great ideas about improving their processes, some of which might involve significant investment. It is common however to see their grand plans quashed when it comes to getting permission or financial backing. Improvement ideas can sound as requests for new toys and observations can appear as complaints.

In addition, a team that presents an improvement idea without framing it within a business case is less likely to be funded by the people who control the budgets. This might either be because the business stakeholders don't understand the value proposition or they just might not take it seriously, because it is not written in their language.

If the team is not given feedback as to why their idea was not funded, and have further requests turned down, they may think 'they will never go for that' and not even mention the next big idea. If this happens frequently, potentially great ideas will be dismissed in favour of those that require much less investment but that are also much less likely to provide equivalent results.

If an improvement idea needs investment of any significant amount, then it is likely to be necessary to convince an internal stakeholder, quite possibly from outside the IT department, that it is a sound investment. If teams present improvement ideas with a business case they will have a much higher success rate.

Instead of asking for open-ended time and investment, present a likely return within a reasonable time period, with an appropriate amount of associated risk.

Key benefits

Just going to the effort of quantifying the opportunity might be enough. Often the potential benefit far outstrips any cost and there is no need to go any further in creating a business case.

Going beyond quantification and producing a full business case will make it easier to get funding for improvement ideas. This is for several reasons:

- Business cases prompt people to offer a rational response to a request by presenting information in a format that is easy to understand.
- They information is in the format that business people can use to make investment decisions.
- Finally and most importantly, they present ideas as likely outcomes: If I invest x, then I get y.

Business cases are versatile; they can be used throughout the organisation (and probably already are). We think that teams can use them for improving their way of working in the same way that whole departments can use them to fund a large change initiative. After all, businesses are built around the successful use of this technique.

How to make it work

At one of our financial services clients, the team calculated the break-even point in time savings for investing in automating regression testing. The department had an application with an ever-growing manual regression test pack that was taking around 100 person days to run per release. The team estimated the total effort to automate the testing at about 240 person days. It was then simple to calculate the break-even point as 3 regression pack runs, so the team put this business case in front of the head of department who immediately chose to fund the improvement.

This simple calculation did not even take into account the opportunity to reduce risk through task automation. When compiling a business case, consider including the risk angle. The decrease in risk can be significantly more important than the explicit value.

Another way to make this work well is to provide several options. Having multiple options to compare and contrast not only increases the chance of success, but may itself also increase the likelihood of a decision to select one of them. As Alan Weiss explains in *Million Dollar Consulting* regarding selling choices to clients, 'always provide options – a choice of yeses'.

In order to compare investment opportunities we need to relate them back to the same currency. For example, asking someone to choose between something that will take about a week and an alternative that costs $10,000 is unhelpful.

In a business with limited investment capital, different parts of an organisation compete for the same capital. Teams who can describe an opportunity in a concise business case will find win the lion's share of investment decisions.

A word of warning: as with any other business case, the assumptions included when formulating the plan will be tested. If a team makes unfounded assumptions that exaggerate their business case, then they may find future business cases reviewed with a much higher diligence. Remember the boy who cried wolf.

We've known teams who say that they cannot be certain about the likely cost of investment or the likely benefits to be realised; the result is that they do nothing. Instead we encourage teams to be brave. A plan is not a contract, it is an improvement idea and its primary purpose is to aid a conversation. By creating a business case, teams make the assumptions explicit. They have the chance to openly discuss our assumptions with colleagues and those in charge of the money.

With investment cases, teams are asking their internal stakeholders to use their business experience to judge proposals. Once people start framing improvement opportunities in terms of costs and benefits, they are often surprised at how engaged their partners become in selecting investment opportunities.

LOOK AFTER THE PENNIES

Teams transitioning to agile methods have to make major changes and sustain significant improvements in order to be able to frequently ship a high-quality product, such as automating testing and deployment. Once some of the obvious improvements have been made, it becomes harder to find further significant improvements. When this happens improvement efforts can become stifled, teams that continue to concentrate on finding big improvements may pass over smaller but easy-to-implement changes, in search of the holy grail. As Monty Python taught us, the grail is very hard to find, involving killer rabbits and knowledge of the airspeed of an unladen swallow.

Those of a lean persuasion often talk about embedding a kaizen culture, meaning one of continuous, small, improvements. In practice however, many teams we see are mostly hunting down the woolly mammoths of improvement ideas (kaikaku in Japanese).

If we only consider the big stuff, the logical conclusion could be that there aren't any improvements left that are within our sphere of influence. We might stop running experiments, stop holding retrospectives or maybe even stop working on improvement tasks altogether. Unless continuous improvement becomes fully baked into the team's culture and ways of working, there is a serious risk of stagnation.

Look after the pennies and the pounds will look after themselves. This adage fits the little and often kaizen culture. Don't look for a knockout punch – instead make frequent, small but consistent changes giving you marginal gains. This can lead to a large overall improvement, in a short time.

Sir Dave Brailsford, the man behind the British track cycling and Team Sky's Tour de France successes in recent years, is hailed as a master of this approach. He described it as, *'If you broke down everything you could think of that goes into riding a bike, and then improved it by one percent, you will get a significant increase when you put them all together'*. His teams worked at improving every single item or activity that went into executing a race or tour, from bike and athlete to the pillows they used.

It is worth pointing out that they didn't optimise one thing in isolation, ignoring the overall goal of winning the race. For example, they didn't optimise the time in which the equipment driver could get between stage checkpoints, only to find he had set off for the next stage end point before the cyclists had finished the previous one.

The main lesson from this story is that even the smallest improvements can add up. Anything is fair game for improvement, so don't limit what you consider.

Key benefits

Looking for the one-percent items results in great new improvement ideas. Team members will be surprised just how many they collect when they are looking out for them.

A well organised pot of small improvement items can be used to build an argument for negotiating lower levels of work commitment. This pot of small items also allows a team to fill any slack with improvements that can be squeezed in easily.

Using small improvements to perform a lightweight and focused retrospective is as simple as deciding which of them to try and implement in the coming iteration.

A group of small improvements will very quickly equal or surpass in benefit previous large improvements that stakeholders view as significant. Resolving the small issues and collecting the completed ones has a motivational effect on the team, as they start to see the combined effect of improvements over time.

How to make it work

Find a way to bake those pennies into the team's way of working. This means finding a low cost-to-collection method as well as finding a trigger to remind people to propose ideas.

Remembering to catch the small improvements is mostly about the routine. A good place to start is the daily stand-up. Finish it with a quick round-robin of anything you did or want to do. Some teams like to capture ideas in an electronic form, but if the proposals are not immediately visible, they often do not get done.

A good visible way of capturing the items is to create some virtual one-percent pots on a white board, one for to-do items and the other for done items. Whenever you think of a small improvement, write it down on a sticky note and put it up in the 'to-do' pot. When you next run a retrospective, you will have a group of ideas that the team could use as input, theming and prioritising for selection as actions to address. When you complete a small improvement, move the sticky note to the 'done' pot. This can be rewarding, like collecting loose change

in a bottle at home. Look through the 'done' pot over several retrospective periods. You might see trends, either in the types of improvements or simply in the total completed in a period.

As the pot of done items grows, it is worth measuring the results. Measuring improvement of a specific change is great, but remember that, as with the Olympians, the desired outcome is an improvement to the whole. For example, by all means measure an improvement in automated test coverage, but also measure extrinsic quality or risk coverage in some way.

ISOLATE EXPERIMENTS

MONDAY	TUESDAY	WEDNESDAY	THURSDAY	FRIDAY
✗	✓	✗	✓	✗

Mr Jay-Z said 'I've got 99 problems'. Haven't we all? Most teams that we work with certainly feel like there are more than enough problems to solve. It might be tempting to try more than one improvement idea at any one time, in the hope of solving more problems faster. After all, who wouldn't want to give themselves a fighting chance?

But beware – trying too many improvement ideas at once in itself creates problems. Firstly and probably most significantly, it makes it very hard to attribute results to a particular improvement idea. Remember secondary school (we know that it probably feels like a million miles away now), and then recall one of the most important principles of practical science: constrain variables and vary one to see its effect.

Fortunately (or unfortunately depending on your view) software teams do not work in an environment where this is possible. It is very hard to repeat experiments while controlling variables in the software delivery environment – we certainly don't spend our time in climate-controlled laboratories. If we try too many improvement ideas at once, how do we tell if we should continue with all of them, drop some or even stop all of the proposed changes?

Imagine a simple situation: we run two experiments A and B at the same time. At the end of the iteration, the chosen measure, for example velocity, has improved 20%. The natural conclusion is that we should keep both these ideas.

However, there are a couple of possibilities. Both ideas might increase velocity, A by 12% and B by 8%. The conclusion is, as before, that both A and B are useful. Or, idea A might decrease velocity by 10%, while idea B increased it by 30%. In this instance, it would make sense to drop A and only keep B, resulting in a total increase of 30%.

We are sure that you can extrapolate this further. If you are thinking of running five or ten experiments, it would be very hard to reach any conclusion about an outcome.

Secondly, by trying to tackle too many problems at once, we increase our work in progress (WIP). Evidence from lean practice tells us that increasing WIP is a very natural behaviour when faced with a long backlog of things to tackle. It is also a recipe for disaster, as people start way too much and not finish anything.

So the solution is simple in theory: don't try to solve too many problems at the same time. In practice, this is easier said than done. The general idea is to limit the number of improvement ideas that people try in any one iteration.

Key benefits

Trying out fewer improvement ideas at one time gives teams the benefits associated with a lower work in progress, such as lower lead times and higher throughput.

Limiting the number of experiments gives the team a clear continuous improvement focus for the iteration. This is likely to vastly improve the chances of completing the experiments.

When a team tries fewer ideas at the same time, they can be more confident in the conclusions from the improvement experiments. In turn, they are likely to make better choices about process changes. People are less likely to inadvertently implement a process handbrake, thinking that it was in fact an accelerator.

How to make it work

There is nothing complicated about isolating experiments. It all comes down to discipline. In short, stop starting and start finishing. At the end of each retrospective, you will probably have many potential improvement ideas. Limit how many you choose to take away and execute.

You don't necessarily have to limit yourself to only one concurrent experiment, although we have worked with many teams who have applied this rule successfully. Returning to our school science analogy, you are unlikely to be able to control all the variables.

To curb the effect of experiment cross-contamination, pick the ones that are likely to affect different parts of the system. Before the systems thinkers amongst you object, we say this acknowledging that teams work in very complex systems where seemingly unrelated factors can have surprising effects. So our advice is this: be sensible, don't choose things that are obviously interconnected and will render the results ambiguous, and be on the lookout for connections between experiments.

BAKE IMPROVEMENTS IN

For teams who have an established retrospective cadence, one session and its outcomes can blur into all the others. If we do not take the time to review and acknowledge the success or failure of improvement ideas, we are likely to lose track of what has worked and what has not.

This could prove very costly for the team in the long run – members might lose out by failing to capitalise on beneficial changes of practice. It is possible that they could end up trying the same improvement idea again or at least something very similar that has or hasn't worked in the past.

We can imagine that many of you reading this now will be saying, 'Ben, Tom, don't be silly, that would never happen to us, of course we would remember'. Okay, now take a moment to recall your last three improvement ideas or experiments. Even if you can recall them now (you didn't remember them all, did you?), do you recall them on a daily basis as you go about your team work?

Any successful team has likely experimented with many improvement ideas, and it would be wasteful to forget the outcomes of those experiments. To protect against this, we recommend doing a couple of things:

- Keep a list on display of all the improvement ideas that did not yield the result you expected or even made things worse. At the very least, this is a great visual aid for your team and those surrounding you, showing your continual commitment to improvement and learning, but in addition it also acts as a list to check against when you are generating future ideas.

- For those items that were successful, bake them in to your working processes. Luckily, technical improvements are automatically preserved. For example, a change to the build pipeline stays there until someone actively removes it. For other types of improvements, people have to make an effort to bake them into the process.

Key benefits

Assessing what improvements to bake in and making sure the effort is sustained is critical. We don't want to lose the gains, particularly after the effort to bring them about in the first place.

Without a feedback loop it is impossible to understand whether and how much we have improved. Ultimately, seeing changes for the better helps us to maintain motivation. This simple act of acknowledging success or failure is critical to driving your team's continuous improvement effort.

Creating the lists stops teams repeating the same old experiments and ensures that those that worked become engrained in the team's way of working.

How to make it work

Next time you have a retrospective, after you have established a safe environment and checked in, review the outcome of your last improvement idea or experiment. Having concrete measures of success will make this a lot easier, allowing you to review whether the needle moved in the right direction. As a side note here, we should point out that using a balanced

portfolio of measures, including some holistic ones, will help catch any other unanticipated effects. Make sure to review those holistic numbers alongside your specific experiment measures.

If the idea worked well, then it might seem obvious to continue with it (whether quantitative or qualitative in nature), but it is worth confirming the collective view of the team in order to cement the idea as a new standard way of working. Once you've reviewed it, write it down, regardless of the outcome. As we mentioned earlier, collecting unsuccessful ideas in a list and displaying them in the team space is a good way to celebrate the learning gained from ideas that didn't work out.

For those improvements that turn out to be successful but are not automatically applied, we recommend baking them into your team way of working. This could be done in a few ways. One way is in the form of a written team charter. The team charter is like having a quick reference guide to how you operate. It is a prompt

to refer to when stuck amongst the trees, unable to see the wood. Another way might be adding it as a criterion to the Definition of Done, a checklist of engineering quality standards that must be met generically for any given work item.

This is particularly important for behavioural changes that you might try to initiate. It is hard to get buy-in from all team members for behavioural changes, because these changes require considerable effort. It's easier to stick with the status quo. So when you get an agreement to try a behavioural improvement idea, and it is shown to be a success, don't let people go back to the old ways. All too often we have seen teams try hard for the next iteration and get great results, only to let things slip once the spotlight is off. Write the idea down, print it off and take it with you into team sessions, regularly citing the agreement when you need it. Achieving sustained behavioural change is really tough and requires continual reminding, often until well beyond when people think it has become baked in.

IMPROVING OUTCOMES

TASK OUT IMPROVEMENT IDEAS

Sometimes teams don't bother to write down the actual tasks necessary to implement the ideas they come up with in retrospectives.

Not having specific tasks against an improvement idea makes it hard to understand the likely effort to complete it and to justify prioritising it. A team board might have many other clearly defined and executable tasks, and the team members will naturally be tempted to tackle these ahead of any work related to a vague improvement idea.

In addition, teams who fail to take the time to task out their improvement ideas can often miss the opportunity to create a shared understanding. Failing to drive out the ambiguity leads to confusion and even competing efforts that cancel each other out and certainly introduce waste.

Even teams that build a shared understanding during the retrospective can struggle to remember exactly what they agreed on, once outside the session and back under pressure to deliver.

Make sure that your team not only identifies improvement ideas but also tasks them out. When the team leaves the retrospective and returns to the hubbub of their working environment, having the ideas documented, visible and with tasks specified is often the only way to make sure they get done.

Key benefits

Tasking out your experiment will drive better outcomes. As any team who tasks out their user stories will attest, this action encourages a good degree of clarity. It forces the team to consider not only what they would like to achieve but how they are going to go about making it happen.

When done as a whole team it drives collaboration to find a better improvement idea than any one individual would come up with by themselves.

By tasking out the improvement idea it also allows the team to better understand the likely cost of the improvement idea. As discussed in *Create a business case,* this will help the team get investment by providing information that they might use in a business case.

A further consequence is that each member of the team is very clear about exactly what is required to execute the improvement idea. It is not uncommon for team members to agree enthusiastically to what has been said at the time, only to realise that they understood different things once the idea is written down or articulated with examples. This factor alone will lead to a marked improvement in the completion of your improvement ideas.

Finally, a set of visible tasks act as a continual prompt of the importance of improvement. It helps remove the reliance of the team on any one person by reminding them of their commitment directly.

How to make it work

Task out improvement ideas in much the same way as you would task out user stories. Even estimate them if that will help you include them in your forecasted work. Make sure you allot necessary time at the end of your retrospective session to do this, 15 minutes should be enough. Write the tasks on sticky notes or whatever you use to visualise tasks on your regular stories. Then manage them as you would any other tasks on your board.

We once worked with a team who had had long discussions about bolstering test coverage in some risky areas. During stand-up a couple of days later a team member said, 'Yesterday I set up Cucumber and started wiring up a test'. A couple of team members listened in disbelief before interjecting 'That isn't what we agreed to'. After team members had expressed a fair amount of disgruntlement and confusion, it turned out that they had come away from the discussions with completely different interpretations of what had been said. Half the team thought they were adding acceptance tests in Cucumber, the others thought they were adding unit tests in their existing tool, JUnit. It was only when they took the time to discuss the specific tasks they thought were required that it became evident there was a mix-up. In this case the confusion was not costly, but the potential for waste here is huge.

Teams may often end up with a bunch of technical tasks to execute to complete their improvement idea. However not all improvement ideas are technical. Some are about lobbying business stakeholders for bigger changes. In these cases you are likely to have tasks like 'Go and speak to Joe about our prioritisation process' or 'Create a business case for faster computers'. These are valuable tasks – don't be constrained to only documenting technical tasks.

A belt-and-braces approach to help you increase completion of improvement ideas is to assign a specific responsible person. This person is responsible for reminding the team of the importance of implementing the idea and the commitment they made to continuous improvement. We have seen teams do this successfully at the idea level and even down to the task level. However, remember that if you do this at the idea level, this person is not the person responsible for executing the improvement idea – it remains the responsibility of the whole team.

TEST ASSUMPTIONS WITH SMALL EXPERIMENTS

Quite often teams aim for the stars, and rightly so. However, large improvement ideas come with large costs, and the larger the cost the larger the degree of risk. If this risk is not sufficiently managed, it can lead to undesirable outcomes. Either the investment doesn't lead to the forecast improvements or the investment keeps growing in pursuit of the desired gains.

Different investments might involve different types of risk, even if they have similarly large amounts of money involved. We might quickly test a hypothesis that removes most of the associated risk, leaving us to incrementally roll out the rest of the investment. On the other hand, we might need to continually test different aspects of the hypothesis by dividing our improvement idea into chunks.

Large assumptions and increased risk are nothing new. Part of the appeal of agile principles and methods is that they set out to address both of these issues. All else being equal the amount of risk associated with implementing a proposed solution is proportional to the rate of investment in that solution and the length of time before we prove or otherwise disapprove its validity. As the total amount of investment in an improvement idea increases, so does the risk in the underlying assumptions. Knowing that assumption is the mother of all muck-ups, effort spent on the validation of assumptions pays dividends.

Mistakes as a result of invalid assumptions increase wasted effort and dent the willingness of sponsors to back future improvement ideas.

Providing funds for costly improvement ideas requires a much larger upfront commitment from your sponsors, so it's a big effort to ask for the funds in the first place. The effort in asking for small amounts of investment is much less because it is much easier to get authorisation for lower amounts. Although you have to ask for smaller amounts more often, the total effort involved is less than asking for one large lump sum.

For those already using business cases to get buy-in to your improvement ideas this will be a welcome progression. Instead of asking for a larger investment, seek to find the smallest possible chunk of your idea. As Eric Ries champions in *The Lean Startup*, we should be aiming to complete small experiments to test the hypothesis and de-risk investment.

Key benefits

Asking for a small investment attracts less attention and there is less potential waste. The level of due diligence required for a smaller investment is disproportionately lower than for a larger one. This makes the transaction cost of the funding lower, which means that you will have more time to spend delivering and less time proving that your improvement idea is a worthy investment.

Splitting the improvement into many smaller ones, which still test the main hypothesis, reduces the risk. If you ask for funding for an experiment that will test your hypothesis in four weeks, rather than six months, your incremental risk is much less.

Rational economic decision-makers apply this thinking in order to protect their financial capital. This also applies in situations where a stakeholder wishes to protect their political capital by not staking their reputation on a single big bet.

How to make it work

Start by splitting the improvement idea. Find a split that will provide the most useful feedback about whether the hypothesis and business case are viable and how risky or rewarding further investment is likely to be.

Split your improvement idea into independent parts, making sure that each one has a measurable impact and benefit, and contributes to a larger goal where appropriate. A hedge fund client of ours did this successfully for the automation of a regression test pack. They were considering an investment of $100,000 with a projected saving of $425,000 of time in the first 12 months following the completion of the automation. After they had split the regression pack into smaller chunks, the first part of the pack was estimated to cost $12,000 and save $80,000 of effort. This was the highest-risk, largest-manual-effort part of the regression test suite. When this part of the pack had been automated the effort saving was the equivalent of $74,000. This first success proved that the automation proposal could return more than six times the investment in the first year and made the case for funding further rounds of automation much more compelling.

For improvement ideas which are hard to split and still provide value, identify the assumptions underlying the idea and rank them by risk (try something like the cost of being wrong multiplied by the uncertainty surrounding it). Take the riskiest assumption and ask for funding to test its contribution to your larger goal. If this assumption is proven correct move on to the next, testing each in turn until the hypothesis behind the improvement opportunity is proven one way or another. If the hypothesis turns out to be incorrect, we re-evaluate the idea and choose whether to continue or curtail our investment at the earliest opportunity.

DON'T BATCH YOUR RETROSPECTION

Many development teams live their agile life in a scrum-like time-boxed environment. Amongst the official ceremonies is the retrospective, usually coming at the end of the cycle as punctuation between sprints and allowing the team to review the sprint just ended and identify ways to improve. But what happens if teams choose not to use fixed iterations any longer? What if teams feel that batching identifying improvements into one session every couple of weeks actually impinges on their ability to continuously improve?

A great many of us have experienced the situation where the pressure to deliver something has resulted in the retrospective getting cancelled or delayed. Often it seems easier to lose the short-term cost of the retrospective (but also the long-term benefit), than to delay the other pressing issue. This effect seems, to us, to be most pronounced when teams are using a flow-based approach such as kanban where there might not be a standing expectation to have retrospectives. Here pressure is continuous and without countermeasures, the need to hold retrospectives and pay attention to improvement can be overlooked.

When teams first move away from fixed time-based iterations, we recommend retaining a regular cadence to retrospectives, even if other activities become less regular. At the minimum, this is our timetabled opportunity to improve.

However, continuous improvement is just that: a process of continuously inspecting and adapting the way we do things. To that point, many successful teams we've seen retrospect on-demand while events are still fresh in the members' minds.

Key benefits

For teams moving from time-based iterations to a flow-based approach, keeping regular retrospective sessions at first is a good idea, to ensure the continued focus on improvement. The team's long-term health is sustained and not deferred or overlooked because of continuous pressure to deliver.

If the team expects that retrospective sessions will happen at a regular interval, it is much easier for people to take a break from the never-ending stream of things that must get done right this moment. The result is much better discipline and ultimately fewer missed retrospectives for the team.

Beyond that, some very driven teams we've worked with gained significant benefit from taking time out to immediately review and retrospect when issues and challenges arise.

At its most simple, retrospecting immediately means benefiting from improvement sooner. Why should a team wait until the next retrospective if they could benefit from improvement ideas right now? A change implemented now could save days or weeks of problems compared to what would happen if it was delayed to the next retrospective.

By taking the time to retrospect immediately after significant events, the team can ask the tough questions and get answers while the events are fresh in people's minds, and make sure that they learn from them.

With continuous retrospection, teams need to gather much less data and root cause analysis is much more focused because of the freshness of events. You may have heard the adage 'Too busy chopping the tree to stop and sharpen the axe', supposedly derived from something that Abraham Lincoln said, well, this is the team's opportunity to buck that trend.

How to make it work

If your team is moving to a continuous flow model such as kanban, or is already there, then ensure that you not only retain your retrospective cadence but that you have a recurring diary entry in your calendars. Having the established session in the diary is often all that is needed to ensure that the team retains the discipline required for retrospective sessions.

For teams that would like to avoid batching up improvement opportunities, try using an on-demand approach to retrospectives. A nice way to do this is to drive them from specific needs or events. Use triggers, such as a production issue, after a spike, when someone has learnt something worth sharing, on completion of a particular piece of work or when an assumption turns out not to be true. Having these will reduce the reliance on an individual such as the scrum master to ensure that the team retrospects.

At the least, the team may want to have a prompt at their team board so that when they next stand up, they ask themselves if there was anything they should retrospect on from the previous day. The flexibility that this approach affords means that retrospectives can take minutes rather than hours.

Again, a word of warning, this requires real team discipline. It is all to easy to say 'we will do one later' or 'we will do one next week'. Before you know it, it has been weeks or even months before the team have taken the time to sharpen the axe. This will make chopping wood much harder.

The blended approach is recommended for most teams. Keep the diary entry for the retrospective cadence but look for opportunities to retrospect immediately using the prompts mentioned in the on-demand approach. Once the diary entry pops up in the team members' calendars, the team can judge if they have spent enough time on improvements already or if they should take this formal opportunity to get in a room and retrospect.

CHECK OUT AS WELL AS IN

Most retrospectives end with actions, increased energy and the odd whoop. Just ending the session by noting down the actions misses out on a valuable feedback loop on the effectiveness of the session and how it might be improved upon. Even if the facilitator thinks the retrospective went well they might only have their opinion which might not match the opinion of those in the group.

We once worked with a facilitator at a mobile application company and as an interesting exercise we had her solicit written feedback from the team at the end of the retrospective session. At the same time we asked the facilitator to write down her own feelings about what had gone well and what could be improved. Then we compared the two. The results were very enlightening, not only had the facilitator been more negative about the session than the team but she had highlighted 'lack of fun' as her main concern. This was in direct contrast to most participant feedback who thought 'drive towards actions' was lacking.

At your next retrospective try finishing off by formally checking out. Solicit specific feedback on how well the retrospective was received and how it could be improved for next time.

Retrospect on your retrospective!

Key benefits

Checking out provides the opportunity for the facilitator to inspect and adapt the way they run retrospectives. This allows them to improve so that their participants get more value from future sessions.

Our personal experience has shown us that continuous improvement is hard work and can be seen as a discipline in its own right. Formally checking out is an opportunity for the facilitator to lead by example. By soliciting feedback and making adjustments they demonstrate the process of continuous improvement.

Soliciting feedback straight away, before the retrospective ends, is best. The feedback is freshest, which means that it is most likely to be accurate, genuine and forthright.

How to make it work

Consider what feedback you want to collect and how to go about collecting it. If you are short of time, try asking participants to drop a token in a box after the session, to vote on whether it was good, bad or indifferent. Some conferences collect feedback on talks in a similar way. It is quick and cheap and can be particularly useful if repeated, to see patterns.

People's opinions on retrospective effectiveness are not binary though. If you have more time, try to collect more detailed feedback. Consider the participants and judge for yourself how much detail to solicit. There is a trade-off between the amount of detail you can ask for and adversely affecting opinion by asking for too much effort to provide the feedback. No one wants to be detained for fifteen minutes at the end of a session answering question 117 of a feedback survey.

As a facilitator, consider leaving the room so as not to inhibit the process. Some people don't like to give open criticism, however constructive.

Consider open versus closed questions, the latter are quicker but need to be very concise to be useful. The former take longer to complete and are hard to compile into a statistical form but provide richer feedback.

Examples of questions we tend to ask are:

- *Open:* which parts worked best and which could be improved?
- *Closed:* did we abide by our principles?
- *Open:* use one word to describe the retro?
- *Closed:* have your feelings changed about any subject as a result of this retro?
- *Closed:* did we discuss the most important topic for team improvement?

Try using a scale of 1-10 in order to get quantitative feedback. Each individual tends to have their own default score so you might need to run this over a period of time to normalise the values or just use averages.

There are several different ingredients that make up a retrospective that we can ask for feedback on. Consider the level of individuals' engagement in the retrospective, the depth of analysis undertaken, the amount and quality of insights generated, the enjoyment and energy created, the quality of output, the improvements sustained as a result and how people valued the use of their time for the session.

If you keep soliciting feedback after each of your retrospectives then you will be able to measure their effectiveness over time by looking for patterns of what works and what doesn't. Use the same bank of questions at the end of later retrospectives to allow you to compare the responses directly.

Running through the feedback after the session will point towards those areas to tweak for next time and inform your choice of retrospective process. As a facilitator you can start to adapt to that feedback and change both your own style and the content and format.

Lastly, you may wish to log the feedback received formally so you can refer back to it and analyse it. As we suggested in *Keep switching your process,* keeping a notebook of processes and their success is valuable to inform your choice of formats for future retrospectives.

DESIGN EXPERIMENTS WITH GOAL-QUESTION-METRIC

Retrospectives can generate a lot of improvement ideas, often too many to implement all at once. When teams decide on improvement ideas without a clear strategy, they might waste time working on low-value areas and find it hard to justify the time spent. This could damage their credibility with stakeholders. On several occasions we've seen stakeholders start to closely scrutinise time spent on process improvement ideas, because a team has been unable to demonstrate the value of these experiments. Some have even strong-armed the team into allocating more work to their iterations to keep members busy and stop them from 'playing around'. This raised utilisation to unhealthy levels, reducing both the teams' ability to improve and their overall productivity.

Overall goals are useful to align improvement efforts, because they set an expectation regarding what is important. However, goals can be ambiguous – particularly without clear measures of success. At the same time, choosing a good metric to prove a goal is not easy. Sometimes the goal is very hard to measure, may not be directly observable or may be holistic and subject to the interaction of many complex variables. There is an old adage, that anything measured improves. However, if the chosen metric is a poor proxy for the goal, getting a better figure will not move the team towards the goal. Choosing the wrong metric might also trigger undesirable behaviour such as local optimisations to the detriment of the overall organisational goals, or attempting to game the metric.

Rather than define metrics from the bottom up without a target, drive them top down from goals. Run a retrospective to work out the metrics that best validate a goal, by using the *Goal Question Metric* method. GQM was originally used by Victor Basili to evaluate defects for projects at the NASA Goddard Space Flight Center, but it can be applied more generally to any goal. It aims to tie a *conceptual goal* to an *operational level* (specific team context) through questions whose answers are at the *quantitative level* in the form of data (metrics).

Key benefits

The GQM method requires teams to first establish a set of goals, which provides focus for improvement ideas. Basili's method promotes direct questioning of the purpose and motivation for a goal. This discussion helps to reshape and sharpen the goal and remove ambiguity. Questioning the goal also helps to establish the most appropriate validation metrics, and ensures that the chosen objectives are related to the selected goal measurements.

Involving a delivery team in questioning the goals, and deciding on the right measurements, improves the team members' understanding of the purpose behind the goals. People have the chance to contribute to the overall objectives, so they will feel responsibility for following through with the necessary actions.

How to make it work

Start by writing up the goal. The GQM model provides a structure to write down goals in a specific and contextual form. Declare an *object* that the goal relates to (for example 'product releases'), then assert an *issue* or attribute you want to impact (for example 'the number of failing') and a *purpose*, the way in which you want to impact the issue (for example, 'reduce'). Lastly add a *viewpoint* ('from an end user's perspective'). For example, a full GQM goal definition might be 'Reduce the number of failing product releases, from an end user's perspective'.

The second step is asking questions that clarify the goal. Define the current state of the *object* and *issue*, within the team's context. That will provide a good indication of how the team is moving in relation to the goal. Remember to do this from the chosen viewpoint. For example, start by asking what constitutes a failing product release from an end user's perspective? This could be based on the number of significant defects discovered by users in production. Spend some time exploring alternative questions to clarify the goal.

Instead of counting defects, teams can measure outages or downtime. Associate one or more metrics with each question, selecting appropriate units for those metrics. For example, a percentage of recent releases with significant defects.

Ask questions and define metrics for each attribute that you consider useful to evaluate the *object*. Remember to keep the stakeholder perspective in mind – better still involve the stakeholders in the process. Consider multiple stakeholders when defining a goal, to avoid optimising for one to the detriment of others. For example, if a team only improves the areas of a product that end-users can see, they could end up ignoring customer services or support, and making it difficult to monitor or inspect product usage.

Our last tip for the GQM method is to consider any behavioural side-effects that might result from the chosen metrics. Investigate what is the easiest way to shift the chosen metric in the intended direction, because that is how teams will likely approach the problem. Consider if the actions the teams might take are desirable and fit in with the overall organisational goals. One company we worked with set the goal of improving the throughput of development teams. Once the teams had worked out the benefits of maintaining a stable work-in-progress limit, some decided that an easy way to increase throughput was to reduce the size of work items, and reduce the lead time of each item. When people considered this side-effect, they agreed that work items were often too large, so breaking them up was a good behaviour. The teams also quickly realised that not all ways to break up the items were good. For example, breaking up items on technical boundaries could lead to potentially unwanted behaviour, because it would shorten the lead time for each item but delay shipping overall functionality to end-users.

MAKE IMPROVEMENTS YOUR NUMBER ONE

Plans made during our retrospective sessions can evaporate as soon as the heat of delivery sets in. Agreeing with stakeholders that continuous improvement is first-class work is not the biggest challenge. The discipline to keep delivering improvements alongside other work is much harder to maintain.

Failure often sets in when not all team members understand the importance of the improvement idea. They may nod and agree during the retrospective, but when it comes to implement it they have little idea what it is about, why they are doing it or how they will know when they have completed it.

Finally, another common reason that our plans go awry is that implementing improvement ideas is hard work. They often involve fixing some of the toughest problems, and the work might not deliver immediate benefits and praise at first, whereas when we hand over working software we get these nice results immediately. Under time pressure it is easy to choose immediate benefits over long-term improvements.

In order to make sure your improvement idea gets done, make it number one by putting it explicitly at the top of your team board.

Key benefits

The action of putting your improvement at the top of your team board is a statement of intent. It tells the world and reminds the team that you value your improvement idea as first-class work. It reinforces the determination to get improvements completed within the time-box of a sprint.

Outwardly, this will show your unwavering commitment to improve your delivery process to your business sponsor. In turn, they will be much less likely to ask you to forgo your improvement idea for that iteration if they know it is your top priority.

Inwardly, having the improvement idea at the top of the board will reinforce the commitment you made as a team. Every day at stand-up, it will be the first thing that you discuss, rather than the last, or worse, not discussed at all. As you work your way through the items of work on the board, you will give as much attention to this item as all the other items.

Treating your improvement idea with the same respect you would any other item and starting it first will go a long way to improving your success rate.

How to make it work

At the start of the next iteration, make space at the top of your team board for your improvement idea. If you use swim lanes this is easy. Instead of taking your stories and tasks for the sprint and putting them in priority order on the board, first thing after your retrospective, put your improvement idea in the top swim lane on your board.

After you have put your improvement idea at the top of your board, then fill the rest of your capacity with functional delivery items. This is the direct opposite to the behaviour that we commonly see, where teams commit to functional delivery items first and then see what improvement ideas they can fit in if they have a good sprint.

For those teams using a kanban board, maybe consider putting the improvement idea at the top of your backlog or prioritised queue so that you can pull the item into the next available space in your system. Alternatively we have seen teams use a dedicated class of service for improvement ideas.

We advise a level of discretion at this point. If the improvement idea is likely to offend anyone or be controversial for any reason (be aware that this could be the case even if it causes no offence within your team) then making it public in any way is not advisable.

Continue your daily stand-up as normal, but give the improvement idea as much attention as you would any other item on your board. We have seen teams take this principle to the level where they say what they did yesterday, what they did today and any blockers they have specifically on the improvement idea.

If you are questioned about making the improvement idea number one, try creating a business case and including a summary for justification. We've found that by making this justification visible, people often rank an improvement idea favourably against software deliveries. We find it useful to think of this value in terms of the cost of not doing the improvement idea.

It is now over to you. As with so many improvement practices, success depends on discipline.

BIBLIOGRAPHY AND RESOURCES

- Developmental Sequence in Small Groups, by Bruce W. Tuckman, Psychological Bulletin, ISSN 0033-2909, Vol 63(6), Jun 1965, pp384-399
- The Checklist Manifesto: How to Get Things Right, by Atul Gawande, ISBN 978-0312430009, Picador 2011
- Scaling Lean & Agile Development: Thinking and Organizational Tools for Large-Scale Scrum, by Craig Larman and Bas Vodde, ISBN 978-0321480965, Addison-Wesley Professional 2008
- User Story Mapping: Discover the Whole Story, Build the Right Product, by Jeff Patton, ISBN 978-1491904909, O'Reilly Media 2014
- Peopleware: Productive Projects and Teams, by Tom DeMarco and Tim Lister, 3rd Edition, ISBN 978-0321934116, Addison-Wesley Professional 2013
- Million Dollar Consulting, by Alan Weiss, 4th Edition, ISBN 978-0071622103, McGraw-Hill Education 2009
- Software for Your Head: Core Protocols for Creating and Maintaining Shared Vision, by Jim and Michele McCarthy, ISBN 978-0201604566, Addison-Wesley Professional 2002
- Six Thinking Hats, by Edward de Bono, 2nd Edition, ISBN 978-0316178310, Back Bay Books 1999
- Freedom from constraints: Darkness and dim illumination promote creativity, by Anna Steidle and Lioba Werth, Journal of Environmental Psychology, ISSN 0272-4944, Volume 35, September 2013, Pages 67–80
- Toyota Production System: Beyond Large-Scale Production, by Taiichi Ohno, ISBN 978-0915299140, Productivity Press 1998
- Lead with Respect, by Michael Balle and Freddy Balle, ISBN 978-1934109472, Lean Enterprises Inst 2014
- Project Retrospectives: A Handbook for Team Reviews, by Norman L. Kerth, ISBN 978-0932633446, Dorset House 2001
- Agile Retrospectives: Making Good Teams Great, by Esther Derby and Diana Larsen, ISBN 978-0977616640, Pragmatic Bookshelf 2006
- The Lean Startup: How Constant Innovation Creates Radically Successful Businesses, by Eric Ries, ISBN 978-0670921607, Viking 2011
- How to Measure Anything: Finding the Value of Intangibles in Business, by Douglas W. Hubbard, 3rd Edition, 978-1118539279, Wiley 2014
- The Goal: A Process of Ongoing Improvement, by Eliyahu M. Goldratt and Jeff Cox, 2nd Edition, ISBN 978-0884270614, North River Press 1992
- Goal Question Metric, by Victor R Basili and H. Dieter Rombach, from Encyclopedia of Software Engineering - 2 Volume Set, ISBN ISBN 1540048, John Wiley and Sons 1994
- Thinking, Fast and Slow, by Daniel Kahneman, ISBN 978-0374533557, Farrar, Straus and Giroux 2013
- How Do Committees Invent, by Melvin E. Conway, Datamation magazine April 1968, F. D. Thompson Publications

Online resources

Visit fiftyquickideas.com for quick access to the following resources:

- Technical Debt Quadrants, by Martin Fowler, 2009
  martinfowler.com/bliki/TechnicalDebtQuadrant.html
- Olympics cycling: Marginal gains underpin Team GB dominance, by Matt Slater, BBC Sport, 2012
  www.bbc.co.uk/sport/0/olympics/19174302
- Lean Coffee
  leancoffee.org
- XP Radar Chart, by Bill Wake, 2000
  xp123.com/articles/xp-radar-chart/
- The twelve principles of the Agile Manifesto
  www.agilemanifesto.org/principles.html
- Scrum Checklist, by Henrik Kniberg, 2012
  www.crisp.se/wp-content/uploads/2012/05/Scrum-checklist.pdf
- Ishikawa (Fishbone)
  en.wikipedia.org/wiki/Ishikawa_diagram
- Why are we so illuded? by Arnold M. Zwicky, Stanford University September 2006
  http://web.stanford.edu/~zwicky/LSA07illude.abst.pdf
- You keep using that word, Dan North, from CukeUp 2015
  https://skillsmatter.com/skillscasts/6144-agile-you-keep-using-that-word
- Seven pillars of agile, by Brian Marick, 2009
  http://www.exampler.com/blog/2009/06/10/the-seven-pillars-of-an-agile-team-introduction/

FIFTY
Quick
IDEAS

This book is part of a series of books on
improving various aspects of iterative delivery.
If you like it, check out the other books from
the series at **50quickideas.com**

FIFTY QUICK IDEAS
TO IMPROVE YOUR
USER
STORIES

by Gojko Adzic and David Evans

FIFTY QUICK IDEAS
TO IMPROVE YOUR
TESTS

by Gojko Adzic, David Evans and Tom Roden

Lightning Source UK Ltd.
Milton Keynes UK
UKOW07f1850191216
290384UK00010B/88/P